BEYOND THE DREAM: FULFILLING YOUR PURPOSE

MARVIN ST. MACARY

Beyond the Dream: Fulfilling the Purpose

Copyright © 2025 by Stmacary Innovative Group

All rights reserved. Published in the United States by Stmacary Innovative Group. No part of this book may be reproduced or transmitted in any form or by any means without written permission from the author.

The scanning, uploading, and distribution of this book without permission is theft of the author's intellectual property. If you would like permission to use material from the book, please contact pastormarvin@therampchurch.com.

Thank you for the support of the author's rights.

Stmacary Innovative Group.

701 Thomas Rd., Lynchburg, VA 24502

ISBN: 979-8-9899726 3-0

PRINTED IN THE UNITED STATES OF AMERICA

Book Cover Photographer: Lennaa May (US)

To Eric Johnson—your belief in me was the spark that ignited my journey. As my academic advisor at Fordham University, you not only saw something in me but also gave me the opportunity to step into my future. Your recommendation for my acceptance into Fordham and your advocacy for my internship at Bad Boy Entertainment set me on a path I never could have imagined. Your faith in me changed my life, and for that, I am eternally grateful.

PRAISE FOR MARVIN ST. MACARY

Marvin St. Macary is the encourager of all encouragers, yet he stands as the epitome of triumph in his own story. This book is not just a collection of spiritual reflections and God-moments—it is a testament to his journey, rising through the ranks from Bad Boy Entertainment to becoming an Executive Pastor at one of the most recognized churches in the world, The Ramp Church International. With every page, he proves that perseverance and drive truly pay off. Each prompt challenges you to confront the areas of your journey you've shelved for too long and realize—those days are over!

Pastor Bruce Johnson
    Senior Pastor
    Ramp Church Richmond

CONTENTS

Foreword — vii
Introduction — ix

1. Discovering Your Purpose — 1
2. From Survivor's Remorse to Survivor's Reponsibility — 7
3. Exposure Is Prophetic — 11
4. Put the Pen to the Paper — 15
5. Stop Resurrecting What God Has Already Pronounced Dead — 19
6. Started from the Bottom — 23
7. The Right Posture — 29
8. He's Protecting His Investment — 33
9. Be the Blueprint — 37
10. The Beauty That Pain Produced — 43
11. Make The Cut — 49
12. The Hero to the Story — 53
13. The Power of Agreement — 59
14. Intimacy Precedes Birthing — 63
15. Enemy of Progress — 69
16. The Winds of Purpose — 75
17. Catch the Rhythm — 79
18. I Don't Like the Word Process — 85
19. Are You Willing to Put in the Work? — 91
20. The 4th Watch Crew — 97
21. You Can't Escape It — 103
22. Is it to good to be true? — 109
23. Pivot — 115
24. One Thing — 121
25. Build Up Your Frontline — 127
26. Illuminate the Path — 133
27. I'm In It but It's Not In Me — 139
28. Representation Matters — 145
29. Calculated Faith — 151

30. The Paradox of Perfection: Trusting God Through
    Imperfection   155
31. Unpack Here   161

   Acknowledgments   167
   About the Author   169
   Also by Marvin St. Macary   173

FOREWORD

I first met Marvin St. Macary in 2006, unaware of the profound role he would play in my life and in the lives of countless others. Over the years, I have had the privilege of witnessing his remarkable journey—one defined by transformation, resilience, and an unwavering commitment to his divine purpose. From his early days navigating the entertainment industry to his current role as a preacher, visionary, and leader at Ramp Church International, Marvin's life is a testament to the power of aligning with God's calling.

His journey began at Fordham University, where he developed a deep appreciation for the arts and the pursuit of truth. This period was not just an academic experience but a time of refinement, preparing him for a career that would ultimately blend creativity and ministry in a profound way. His ascent in the entertainment industry—working alongside some of the most influential figures in music, film, and media—seemed to position him for a life of fame and success. Yet, even as he stood at the pinnacle of an industry known for its prestige, God was crafting a greater narrative.

When Marvin responded to the call to ministry, he did not simply walk away from his previous pursuits; rather, he wove them into his greater purpose. As Executive Pastor of Ramp Church International,

FOREWORD

he has spent over a decade investing in others—developing leaders, imparting wisdom, and demonstrating through both word and action what it means to live a life of faith, excellence, and purpose. His ability to merge deep theological truths with practical application is a rare gift, making him not only an extraordinary preacher but also a mentor, strategist, and builder of people.

Beyond the Dream: Fulfilling Your Purpose is not just another book—it is a clarion call to action. Marvin challenges readers to move beyond mere aspiration and take tangible steps toward their God-ordained destinies. Seamlessly integrating spiritual insights with real-world strategies, he equips readers at every stage of their journey with the tools necessary to walk confidently in their calling. This book does not settle for passive inspiration; it is about active transformation.

It is with great honor that I introduce this work, knowing that it will serve as a guiding light for many. Whether you are just beginning your journey, standing at a crossroads, or deep in the trenches of pursuing purpose, this book will challenge, uplift, and propel you forward. Marvin's life exemplifies what it means to move beyond dreams into the reality of a God-ordained destiny.

Marvin St. Macary is more than a pastor—he is a visionary, a bridge builder, and a living testament to the boundless power of faith and perseverance. My prayer is that as you engage with the wisdom within these pages, you will be stirred to embrace your own divine purpose and step boldly into the fullness of what God has designed for you.

Bishop S.Y. Younger

INTRODUCTION

God has a unique and powerful purpose for your life—a purpose that is tailor-made for you, and only you. From the moment you were created, He entrusted you with all the skills and resources necessary for your calling, prebuilt and prepackaged on the inside of you. But here's the thing: His purpose for your life will require you to trust Him, every step of the way. You won't always have the answers, and the path may not always be clear, but it is in learning to trust the voice of God that you will be led to true and complete fulfillment.

Unfortunately, there are so many people in this world who walk through their lives aimlessly; unsure of their purpose or as we like to say, "simply going through the motions." They spend years feeling trapped. Going to a job that they hate, waking up daily with the heavy weight of dread at the thought of even letting their feet touch the floor. With no hope, they are just stuck on the hamster wheel of the routine of life as they know it. But it is my desire to let you know that you weren't created to live a life of mere survival; you were made and designed for something far greater.

I truly believe that you have a billion-dollar concept, an international best-selling book, the most innovative and captivating

INTRODUCTION

ministry, an academy that can shift the industry of education, a cure that can save lives, the strategy that can forever change the face of politics, the invention that will set the new trend in technology, or the movie or the song that will take over the entertainment world! I am convinced that it's all in the kingdom. I refuse to believe that the world is more creative and innovative than we are.

Sometimes we underestimate the power of an idea or a dream. All it takes is one seed! There are so many destinies and legacies connected to the one seed. The power of your yes can unlock doors for nations and generations. Listen to me! Your delay in obedience could be hindering everybody and everything connected to you!

This purpose is not just about you. It's a destiny that you were hand crafted for. A journey, drawing closer to God, depending on Him every moment, and allowing Him to use your life to bless the lives of others. You may feel unqualified. You may even doubt yourself. But I'm here to tell you: You have to do this. Your fulfillment depends on it. The people assigned to you, depend on it. And yes, even the generations that come after you depend on it. God has placed you on this earth for such a time as this, and there are people whose lives will be forever changed because YOU decided to obey. Don't you miss it.

I know it's easy to look at all your inadequacies, all your mistakes, and even your weaknesses, and count yourself out. But God doesn't look at us the way we look at ourselves. He sees the imperfections—and He sees His glory shining through the cracks of our failures. He is the master of using broken vessels. I strongly encourage you to present God with the truth of your brokenness.

In this book, it is my desire to encourage you and walk alongside you as you step into the purpose God has uniquely designed just for you. You may be asking, "*Why me? Why would God choose someone like me?*" Let me ask you this question in return: Why not you?

He's not calling you to show up as perfection; He's calling for what He prepackaged inside what He created. Give him your honesty, your willingness, and your openness and start to function as the carrier of

INTRODUCTION

God's DNA. His Spirit is already within you, so why not partner with Him? With Him, there is nothing that can stop you. What can't you do with God on your side?

This is your time. This is your moment.

Let's work!

1

DISCOVERING YOUR PURPOSE

Purpose is more than just a word—it's the heartbeat of your calling, the fire in your soul, the drive behind your days, and the reason you're still walking this earth instead of resting in heaven. Have you ever wrestled with the question, *"What is my purpose?"* It's a question that lingers in the hearts of many, sometimes remaining unanswered for years.

Some search for purpose in distant places, while others chase it in lofty dreams, grand opportunities, or prophetic words. Often, the answer is right in front of us—hidden in everyday moments or wrapped in the burdens we carry. The truth is purpose doesn't always come as a loud, clear call from the heavens. While it can, more often, it arrives quietly, woven into the fabric of our challenges, struggles, and everyday experiences.

The Burden You Carry May Be Your Calling

Have you ever felt an overwhelming sense of urgency or burden about something? Perhaps you've seen a need—an injustice, a lack of resources, or a broken relationship—and thought, 'Someone should do something.' That someone might be you.

One evening, renowned entrepreneur Jeff Hoffman saw a woman on the news in tears. She ran a homeless shelter on the verge of closing due to a lack of funds. Jeff thought to himself, *"That's unfortunate; somebody should do something."* At that moment, he realized, *"I am that somebody!"*

The next day, he visited the shelter and handed them a check, saving it from closure. How often do we notice a problem and think, *"Someone should do something about it?"* Instead, we should look in the mirror and tell ourselves, *"You are that somebody."*

Your frustration could be pointing to your greatest opportunity. The burdens that weigh on your heart may be the very ones God has called you to carry. That's purpose.

A Divine Call to Action

God often places a burden on our hearts as a doorway into our purpose. It's not meant to overwhelm us, but to serve as a divine call to action. It might be the Holy Ghost's nudge to step into the very purpose He has for you.

Think about it: most of the inventions that have transformed the world began with a person looking at a problem and asking, *"What can I do to fix this?"*

When Ruth Wakefield, the inventor of the chocolate chip cookie, ran out of ingredients for her usual recipe, she didn't quit. Instead, she broke a chocolate bar into pieces and mixed it into the dough—creating an iconic dessert.

Travis Kalanick and Garrett Camp were frustrated with the inefficiency and costs of taxi services. After noticing the problem of waiting for taxis in crowded cities, they created Uber, which revolutionized the transportation industry, making it more accessible, affordable, and convenient for millions worldwide.

Just like these innovators, we are often presented with problems meant to be solved, and the solutions we create could potentially change the world. God places us in specific moments with specific burdens—not for us to ignore them, but to rise to the occasion, seek Him, and provide answers.

So, the next time you encounter a problem, instead of asking, *"Why is this happening?"* ask yourself, *"How can I be the solution?"* Don't stop at the problem.

The Problems You Face May Be Part of God's Plan

It's easy to become discouraged when faced with challenges. Often, the problems that seem the hardest to overcome are the very things that shape our purpose. We tend to view difficulties as obstacles—things to be avoided. But in the Kingdom of God, every challenge has a purpose, and every setback is a setup for something greater.

Think about Moses. He spent years in exile, far from the people he was meant to lead, seemingly forgotten in the wilderness. Then, he encountered a bush that was burning but not consumed—a divine moment that changed the course of his life.

Pastor William Westgate once said, 'Moses was still enough to notice it.' But what if Moses had walked past that burning bush, too distracted by his struggles and uncertainties? He could have missed the very moment God was using to speak to him about his purpose.

In the busyness of life, we often get so caught up in 'doing' that we miss the moments where God is revealing our purpose. We live in a culture of constant activity, and the noise around us can easily drown out the quiet whispers of God. But if we're not careful, we can miss the very moments God is using to speak to us.

God Uses You to Answer the Questions and Solve the Problems

On a routine call with four close friends, we reflected on the struggles young boys in our community face—challenges we once knew firsthand. As we reminisced, we couldn't help but wish that we had possessed the wisdom then that we now hold. Such insight could have spared us from countless missteps and unnecessary detours.

This realization sparked an idea: what if we could bridge the gap by sharing our experiences, offering guidance to those following in our footsteps? From this discussion, *Face to Face: Conversations with My Younger Self* was born—a book designed to impart hard-earned lessons and inspire the next generation.

Every struggle, every experience, and every challenge serves a purpose. God has a divine plan, and He uses our struggles to shape and refine us. The burden you carry, the questions you ask, and the problems you encounter are all pointing you toward your purpose.

Your greatest challenge may be the very thing that propels you into the calling God has for your life. The problems you face are not random; they are often opportunities for God to equip you for the work He has planned. If you remain faithful, you'll begin to see how every seemingly random moment—every struggle, setback, and victory—comes together to reveal the beautiful plan God had for you all along.

So, the next time you face a challenge or feel the weight of a burden, ask yourself: *"How is God using this to reveal my purpose?"* Instead of running from the problem, embrace it. You might just find that the very thing you've been struggling with is the key to unlocking your God-ordained purpose.

Reflection
- What questions have you been asking about your life and calling?
- What burdens or problems stir something deep within you?
- Have you taken the time to seek God's guidance and answers for the things that ignite your passion?

Prayer
Father,
Lord, help me see my struggles through Your eyes. I recognize that You are an intentional God, and even the challenges I face ultimately

are working for my good. Help me to pause and listen for Your voice, so I don't miss the divine moments You have prepared.

Reveal Your purpose for my life, even in the midst of the difficulties I encounter. Give me clarity and understanding as I seek Your guidance, and help me to trust that You are leading me toward the work You've destined for me. Nothing is random with You, Lord. I trust that all things will bring You glory.

In Jesus' name, Amen.

2

FROM SURVIVOR'S REMORSE TO SURVIVOR'S REPONSIBILITY

You Survived!

The trials, the heartaches, the relentless storms—you weathered them all. You made it through. And while you may wonder why you survived when others didn't, here's the truth: your survival is no accident. You survived for a purpose.

There's a fire within you that the enemy couldn't extinguish. Every scar tells a story of resilience. Every tear you shed watered the ground for your next season of growth. Every time you thought it was over, God was at work—positioning, strengthening, and preparing you for what's ahead.

You survived because there is still work for you to do. You survived because your testimony will be the lifeline someone else desperately needs. You survived because your destiny is far greater than your history.

So, stand tall. Walk boldly. Speak with conviction. Love fiercely. Live intentionally. Because your survival is undeniable proof that purpose still calls your name.

Now go, and answer that call.

. . .

Survivor's Guilt

Survivors often grapple with a deep-seated sense of guilt. We look around at those who didn't make it through the same trials, and the weight of their absence can feel crushing. We faced the same struggles, yet God rescued us while others weren't spared. We wonder, "Why me?"

In these moments, it's crucial to remember that your survival wasn't a matter of chance. It wasn't merely a stroke of luck—God has a deliberate purpose for your life after the storm.

Survivor's guilt is real. It creeps in with the haunting thought that maybe you should have done more or been more. But at some point, we must move beyond guilt and recognize that survival is not just a gift—it's a calling. And with the gift of survival, God also entrusts us with a profound responsibility.

Survivor's Responsibility

"Praise be to the God and Father of our Lord Jesus Christ, the Father of compassion and the God of all comfort, who comforts us in all our troubles, so that we can comfort those in any trouble with the comfort we ourselves receive from God."— 2 Corinthians 1:3-4

This passage reveals the purpose behind God's comfort in our suffering. We are called to be extensions of His grace and comfort to those enduring their own struggles. God heals us so that we can help heal others.

If God miraculously restored your marriage when divorce seemed inevitable, it wasn't just for you—it was to equip you to pour into other struggling couples. Your story can demonstrate that no relationship is beyond healing, no matter how broken it may appear.

If God has transformed your life from addiction to a place of freedom and success, it's not only a personal victory—it's a beacon of light for others still trapped in darkness. Your testimony could be the encouragement someone else needs to take their first courageous step toward healing.

Every victory, no matter how personal, has the potential to serve a higher purpose. God uses both our pain and our triumphs to mold us into vessels of encouragement and hope for others. Your life, transformed by His grace, can be a living testament that inspires others to believe that change, healing, and restoration are possible for them, too.

Your miracle is not just for you—someone else is attached to it. You didn't make it through your struggles just to live a comfortable, easy life afterward.

You survived to help others navigate their way through the same battles. Your testimony, your scars, and your victories are not just for you—they are powerful tools to guide others out of the darkness you once knew.

Shift Your Perspective

God calls us to be light in dark places—to encourage, uplift, and guide. But this requires a shift in perspective.

Rather than asking, *'Why did I survive?'* ask, *'How can my survival help others escape their own storms?'*

Surviving isn't the end of the story—it's the beginning of a new chapter where you become an active participant in the healing and liberation of others. Survivor's guilt can become a crushing burden if we allow it to. But when we embrace our survivor's responsibility, we discover purpose in our pain and meaning in our mess.

The tragedy of your breakthrough is if God pulls you out of something, but you never reach back to pull others out. The true blessing isn't found in being the sole survivor; it's in becoming the first of many.

When God delivers you from a struggle, the purpose isn't just your freedom—it's to make you a guiding light for those still trapped.

Your victory paves the way for others to find their own freedom. Your healing sets off a ripple effect of transformation. The blessing truly flows, not when you stand alone, but when you create space for others to step into the freedom you've found.

. . .

Reflection
- How have you witnessed God's faithfulness in your life?
- What lessons from your survival can help others facing similar struggles?
- How can you intentionally shift your perspective from guilt to responsibility and use your story to impact the lives of others?

Prayer
Father,

Thank You for carrying me through the storms. I acknowledge that my survival is not due to my own strength but solely by Your grace. Help me move beyond guilt and fully embrace the responsibility You've given me to help others.

I know my survival is for Your divine purpose. Your Word says we overcome by the blood of the Lamb and the power of our testimony. Lord, allow my testimony to bring unwavering hope to others.

Show me how to use my story, struggles, and survival to guide others to You, helping them find strength and freedom in Your grace.

In Jesus' name, Amen.

3

EXPOSURE IS PROPHETIC

Growing up in an inner-city neighborhood, it's easy to let your reality become confined to the boundaries of your community. It still amazes me how many people in the heart of New York City have never visited a Manhattan museum, attended a Broadway play, or even strolled through Central Park. For many, their world is limited to the familiar streets and routines of their neighborhoods.

One of my greatest childhood blessings was my mother enrolling me in Xavier High School, a prestigious all-boys Jesuit prep school in Chelsea. It was there that I first met students from all walks of life, and it opened my eyes to a world far beyond the one I had known. I was introduced to the arts, particularly theater, and I found myself experiencing the glitz and glamour of New York City in a way I never had before.

As an eighth-grader, I remember riding the trains, observing commuters—especially the men in suits with briefcases, whom I assumed were important. They wore designer neckties and Rolex watches, and I couldn't help but admire them. I wanted to be like them.

Seeing this world up close, I began to believe that one day, I could be part of it too. I started to see beyond the limitations of my current reality, and for the first time, I envisioned a future outside my neighborhood in Jamaica, Queens.

One of the most powerful aspects of walking with God is that He gives us glimpses of His plans for our lives. These moments of exposure—whether through a vision of the future or a prophetic word—are not simply for our entertainment or curiosity.

God doesn't reveal His plans to tease us—He reveals them to prepare us. When God shows us something, it is prophetic—a foretaste of what He is about to do, either through us, in us, or for us.

The Purpose of Exposure

When God reveals something about our future, it is an invitation to partner with Him in the process. Often, the exposure we receive is not fully understood in the moment. It may be a vision of something that seems far off or even impossible, but the very act of God revealing it to us is a declaration of His faithfulness. He is not showing us something just to get our hopes up—He is showing us because He is preparing us for what lies ahead.

In the Bible, we see this principle at work. Consider Joseph. As a young man, God gave him a vision of future greatness—one where his brothers and even his parents would bow before him. This revelation—this exposure—was prophetic, meant to give Joseph a sense of purpose and direction. However, the journey to that destiny was not easy. It involved betrayal, slavery, imprisonment, and many trials.

Despite these challenges, Joseph never forgot what God had shown him. Instead, he trusted that God would bring it to pass.

Exposure Prepares You for the Process

God never reveals something without also preparing us for the journey to reach it. When He gives you a vision or a promise, it is not an instant guarantee that it will come to pass tomorrow.

Exposure is a prophetic declaration that a process is involved. It requires lessons to be learned, character to be develop, and faith to grow. Yet, exposure anchors you to your purpose during the hard seasons.

Just as a farmer plants seeds and nurtures the soil before harvest, God provides glimpses of His work, inviting us to partner with Him in faith and obedience.

Exposure Unveils God's Faithfulness

When God reveals something to us, it is also an unveiling of His faithfulness. He is showing us not just what is to come, but also reminding us that He is the one who brings His promises to fruition.

This is why we must hold tightly to the glimpses God gives us— the dreams, visions, and prophetic words. These are not idle or fleeting; they are the seeds of His promise, waiting to be nurtured by our faith and obedience.

In Jeremiah 29:11, God reassures us:

"For I know the plans I have for you, declares the Lord, plans for welfare and not for evil, to give you a future and a hope."

When God exposes us to His plans, He declares His intention to bring us into the fullness of His will. God's revelations are not just about what we will do—they're about His faithfulness in bringing them to pass.

From Exposure to Fulfillment

Ultimately, exposure is a stepping stone to fulfillment. The glimpses we see, the dreams we are given, and the prophetic words spoken over our lives are all part of God's process of bringing His plans to fruition. We may not understand the timing or how it will all come together, but we can trust that God will complete what He started. In Philippians 1:6, Paul reminds us:

"And I am sure of this, that he who began a good work in you will bring it to completion at the day of Jesus Christ."

God's revelation of His plans is a promise of His faithfulness. What

He exposes to us will not fall to the ground unfulfilled. His plans are certain, and His timing is flawless.

Ephesians 3:20 reminds us:

"Now to him who is able to do immeasurably more than all we ask or imagine, according to his power that is at work within us."

If you can see it or dream it, not only is God faithful to bring it to pass—He will exceed your wildest expectations.

Reflection
- Has God revealed something about your future that you're still waiting to see fulfilled?
- How can you hold on to that exposure in faith while waiting for its fulfillment?
- How can you partner with God in bringing the promises He's revealed to you into reality?

Prayer
Father,

Thank You for the visions, dreams, and prophetic words You've given me. I trust that what You have shown me is a glimpse of what You are about to do in my life. Help me to walk in faith, trusting that You will bring Your promises to pass. Teach me to be patient in the process and obedient to Your leading. I surrender my plans and align with Yours, trusting that Your ways are higher.

In Jesus' name, Amen.

4

PUT THE PEN TO THE PAPER

I used to struggle with remembering my lines when performing in plays. No matter how many times I rehearsed, I would either stumble over words or completely forget key lines. One day, desperate for a solution, I tried a different approach—writing my lines by hand. Surprisingly, this simple shift made all the difference in the world.

There was something almost magical about writing the words down—it created a deeper connection within me. Writing them down made the lines feel more real and meaningful, turning them from mere words on a page into a part of me.

When you feel the stirring of a dream or a deep sense of purpose, one of the most transformative steps you can take is to write it down. In the Bible, God gives us a clear and direct instruction: *"Write the vision and make it plain..."* (Habakkuk 2:2). This simple command is one of the most crucial steps in our journey.

Writing down your vision is an act of faith—it transforms an abstract idea into something tangible. It's the moment when the abstract becomes concrete, and the dream begins to take shape. It marks the beginning of manifesting your idea into reality.

Writing your vision isn't just practical—it's an act of obedience to

God. The simple act of putting pen to paper, or typing your thoughts on a screen, solidifies what God has revealed to you and helps you focus your energy and efforts toward making it reality.

Faith in Action

Having a vision isn't enough; it must be both clear and actionable. Writing it down forces you to crystallize your thoughts, organize them coherently, and make them actionable. God may ignite the vision, but you must take the next step. This is where faith and action come together in a powerful and transformative way.

When you write down your vision, it becomes a bold declaration of faith. You're essentially saying, *"God, I believe with all my heart that You are calling me to this, and I'm going to take this seriously and pursue it with unwavering dedication."* You may not know every detail, but you can trust God to guide every step. When you write your vision down, you're putting your faith into motion and actively partnering with God.

Proverbs 16:3 declares, *"Commit your works to the Lord, and your plans will be established."* When you write down your vision, you are committing your work to God and entrusting Him with your dreams and aspirations. And as you give Him something tangible to work with, He can begin to guide you, refine your plans, and lead you down the precise path He has ordained for you.

Writing helps you process what you believe He's calling you to do and clarifies His specific instructions for you. It's not merely a practical exercise; it's a deeply spiritual one that connects you to the heart of God.

Write It Out and Let God Edit

Writing your vision is not about perfection; it's about obedience to God's call. God is the author of your story, yet He graciously invites you into the creative process. Like any author needs a rough draft,

God delights when you give Him something to shape, refine, and mold into something extraordinary.

What you write today may not be the final version. God will undoubtedly make edits, guide your steps with precision, and may even take your plans in an unexpected direction. But that's the beauty of it all. When you commit your vision to paper, you're creating space for God to take that vision and breathe His very life into it.

It's not about perfection—it's about obedience. Even if what you write feels incomplete or imperfect, writing it down is an offering to God. It's your way of saying, *"Here I am, God, ready and willing to walk in the path You've set before me, trusting that You will equip me for every good work."*

Don't just write your vision once and forget it. Return to it often. Revisit it with intention. Let it serve as a constant reminder of the bigger picture when the day-to-day challenges inevitably arise.

Today, take time to write your vision with intention. Make it clear and direct. Don't let it become a fleeting thought. Put it on paper, commit it to God in prayer, and watch in awe as He takes that small step of faith and transforms it into something extraordinary and beyond your wildest dreams.

Reflection
- Have you intentionally written down the vision God has placed within your heart? If not, take some dedicated time today to prayerfully write it out in detail.
- How does the act of writing down your vision help you step boldly into your God-given purpose and calling?
- Share your vision with a trusted individual and be open to their honest feedback.

Prayer
Father,
Thank You for the dreams and the purpose You've planted in my

heart. Today, I commit to writing the vision You've given me—making it plain, tangible, and actionable. I surrender my plans completely to You. Guide my every step and breathe Your life into the vision. Lord, give me courage to take the first step, trusting You will equip me for every good work.

May this vision bring glory and honor to Your name, and may it inspire and bless others along the way. I surrender my fears, doubts, and uncertainties to You, knowing You are greater than anything I face. I trust in Your perfect timing and unfailing guidance, knowing You will never lead me astray.

In Jesus' name, Amen.

5

STOP RESURRECTING WHAT GOD HAS ALREADY PRONOUNCED DEAD

Thank God He does not conform to the ever-changing rules of people or engage in cancel culture. If He did, I would have been canceled countless times. But God, in His infinite mercy, does not define us by our worst moments. He does not discard us because of our failures, shortcomings, or past mistakes.

God doesn't cancel us, so why do we cancel ourselves? Too often, we carry the weight of our past like a corrupted file stuck on repeat—replaying our mistakes again and again. We allow past failures, regrets, and missteps to hijack our future, convincing ourselves that we are unworthy of grace, unfit for purpose, or incapable of change.

One of the most subtle traps on the journey to discovering and walking in our purpose is the temptation to resurrect the past. But here's the absolute truth: If God has declared something dead, we must stop trying to revive it.

God's Call to a New Beginning

Throughout Scripture, we see time and time again how God extends the invitation for fresh starts. In the book of Isaiah, God speaks through the prophet, declaring:

"Forget the former things; do not dwell on the past. See, I am doing a new thing" (Isaiah 43:18-19).

God tells us with unwavering clarity not to dwell on the past. What's done is done. The mistakes, the regrets, the failures—they are in our rearview mirror. They are buried, and it's time to leave them there.

Too often, our unwillingness to release the past keeps us from embracing the new thing God is orchestrating. We profess to trust Him, yet we stubbornly revisit old wounds, reliving pain that He has already healed. His mercies are new every morning. If God, in His grace, has moved beyond our failures, why do we hold onto them?

Don't Let the Past Be Your Prison

When we cling to the past—especially the shame and mistakes that haunt it—we allow it to become a prison. We relive old wounds, allowing them define our present identity and shape our future. But God has called us to liberation. Who we were is not who we are today, and it's certainly not who God has destined us to become.

We often get ensnared in a futile cycle of trying to "fix" what has already been forgiven or attempting to resurrect relationships, situations, or mindsets that God has already declared dead. This is a dangerous trap. The more we fixate on what God has already handled, the less space we give Him to shape our future.

There is profound freedom in knowing that we don't have to resurrect our past. When we attempt to, we are essentially proclaiming, *"God, what You did wasn't enough."* But His grace is more than enough. His work on the cross was final—'It is finished.'

Let Go and Go Forward

It's time to stop obsessively reliving past mistakes. Every time we replay shame, guilt, or failure, we paralyze ourselves and hinder our ability to step into the future God has designed. Every second we squander resurrecting the past is a second we steal from our future. And that is a cost too high to pay.

Just ask Lot's wife—she looked back at what God condemned, and it cost her everything. The enemy's greatest weapon is keeping us shackled to the past—trapped in regret and fear. But the moment you accepted Christ, those past mistakes lost their grip on you.

Therefore, if anyone is in Christ, he is a new creation; the old has gone, the new is here" (2 Corinthians 5:17).

God is actively doing something new in you. It's time to release the past and embrace the present. Letting go doesn't mean erasing it from your memory—it means consciously choosing not to let it dictate your present or future.

It means accepting God's boundless forgiveness and grace and stepping into your future with the unwavering knowledge that you are not defined by your past. You are defined by God's unconditional love and His magnificent plan for you.

Moving Forward

Walk boldly into the future, without hesitation or regret. The past may have shaped you, but it does not define you. You are not defined by failures, missteps, or shortcomings—you are who God says you are. His love, His grace, and His purpose for your life far outweigh any mistake you have ever made.

God does not hold your past against you, and neither should you. His plans for you are not built on past failures but on His divine promises—promises of hope, restoration, and a future filled with purpose. When you allow your past to dictate your future, you place artificial limits on what God can accomplish through you. But when you surrender your regrets, your fears, and your doubts to Him, you liberate yourself to walk in the fullness of His glorious calling.

Stop letting past wounds, mistakes, and disappointments keep you captive. Instead, embrace the future with open arms and an expectant heart, knowing that God has already gone before you. He has paved the way, opened the doors, and prepared blessings beyond anything you can imagine. Trust in His guidance, step forward in faith, and walk confidently into the future He has prepared for you.

God's best for you is ahead, not behind. The enemy would love for you to believe that your best days are over, but the devil is a notorious liar. Your best days are still ahead.

Keep your eyes fixed on Him, and don't ever look back.

Reflection
- Are there past mistakes or regrets you've been unintentionally resurrecting? How has this affected your progress and peace?
- How can you actively embrace God's boundless forgiveness and transformative grace in your life today?
- What tangible steps can you take, starting now, to move forward into the new and exciting thing God is doing in your life?

Prayer

Father,

I repent for holding on to what You have already forgiven and released. I believe in Your redemptive power and Your transformative word. Help me to release the past and stop resurrecting what You've already declared dead.

I choose to walk in the freedom You have so generously given me, trusting that You are doing a new thing in my life. Infuse me with the strength to leave behind the mistakes, shame, and guilt that have held me captive and to move forward in the unique purpose You have called me to.

I declare freedom from my past and step forward into the future You've prepared for me.

In Jesus' name, Amen.

6

STARTED FROM THE BOTTOM

*P*urpose is found in the places that seem insignificant, roles others overlook, and tasks no one else wants to do. These humble beginnings are where God teaches us invaluable lessons about faithfulness, humility, and preparation for what lies ahead.

At 19 years old, I worked in the school library at Fordham University. Day after day, I found myself in a routine that felt tedious and uninspiring—shelving books, assisting students, and organizing materials. I vividly remember standing among the stacks one afternoon, feeling stuck and unfulfilled. I wanted more. I longed for something purposeful, something that aligned with my calling.

In that moment of frustration, I had an honest conversation with God, voicing my discontent:

"Lord, I don't want to be here. I want to be walking in my purpose. I want more than this."

At the time, I didn't realize God was already working behind the scenes, using that seemingly insignificant season to prepare me for what was ahead.

A few weeks later, an unexpected opportunity arose—I landed an interview for an internship at Bad Boy Entertainment. The role was far from glamorous, and the pay was minimal—just $40 a week, barely enough to cover food and subway fare. Despite the modest paycheck and unimpressive title, I recognized it as a door that God had opened.

It wasn't about the money or the position; it was about the opportunity. I was simply grateful to get my foot in the door.

The work itself was humbling. My days were filled with tasks no one else wanted—answering phones, carrying heavy equipment, picking up lunch, delivering packages, and even walking the CEO's dog. But I made a decision: I was going to embrace this opportunity with gratitude and give it my very best.

Even in those small, seemingly menial tasks, I found joy—not because the work was extraordinary, but because I understood that faithfulness in little things prepares us for greater things.

I learned to serve with excellence, to show up early and stay late, to do my best even when no one was watching.

Step by step, my faithfulness opened new doors, and small tasks led to greater responsibilities. I earned the trust of my superiors, and opportunities that once seemed out of reach started to come my way.

What started as picking up turkey burgers for the CEO at Bad Boy eventually led to sitting in marketing meetings for Allen Iverson's sneaker release and producing music videos for Pharrell.

Looking back, I realize that purpose is never about where you start —it's about how you steward where you are. Every season, no matter how insignificant it seems, is a stepping stone to something greater.

God is always at work, even in the places we don't want to be. Our job is to remain faithful, humble, and ready. That's how purpose unfolds—one step at a time.

The Power of Starting Small

Often, the greatest obstacle to fulfilling your purpose isn't external —it's internal pride.

Pride whispers, *"This is beneath me,"* but humility declares, *'This is an opportunity.'"*

Pride insists, *"I'll wait for something better."* Humility asserts, *"I'll give my best right here and now."*

Many people envision purpose as a grand, fully-formed destiny, yet they resist the process required to reach it. Perhaps your ultimate calling is to pastor, yet you find yourself asked to serve as an usher or an armor bearer. You may aspire to become a CEO, but the journey begins in the mailroom.

The truth is, no role is insignificant when approached with faithfulness. God often tests our character in the hidden places before elevating us to the visible ones.

History and scripture repeatedly show that greatness is often forged in obscurity. Indra Nooyi exemplifies this journey. Before becoming CEO of PepsiCo, she began as a product manager at a small company, steadily working her way up. Through diligence, perseverance, and an unwavering commitment to excellence, she steadily climbed the ranks.

Her story reminds us that no position is wasted when approached with the right mindset. The skills, discipline, and humility developed in the early stages of our careers serve as the foundation for greater impact later.

Before the Throne

But the greatest example of all is Jesus Himself. He didn't start His ministry with a throne; He began in a manger, with carpenter's tools, and years of quiet obedience.

Before performing miracles, teaching crowds, or fulfilling His ultimate purpose on the cross, Jesus spent decades working, learning, and submitting to the process.

Even as He began His ministry, Jesus washed feet before carrying the weight of salvation on His shoulders. His life serves as a powerful reminder that preparation rarely resembles the destination, yet it is essential to reaching it.

Sometimes, all you need to do is get your foot in the door. That door may not look grand, but it is the first step toward what God has prepared for you.

When you embrace humility, every opportunity—no matter how small—becomes a training ground for something greater. Those who are willing to serve in the shadows are the ones God can trust to lead in the light. So, will you despise small beginnings, or will you steward them faithfully?

Seizing the Opportunity

If you feel overlooked, under appreciated, or as if your role doesn't reflect of your potential, take heart. Your faithfulness in these moments is laying the foundation for your future.

Strive to give your all at every level. Excellence is a habit—not a switch you flip when the right opportunity arises. When you work as though you're working for God and not merely for man, every task becomes meaningful.

Practical Steps for Working Your Way Up

1. Show Up with Gratitude

Treat every opportunity as a gift, not an obligation. A grateful heart fosters optimism and motivation.

2. Stay Teachable

Adopt a learner's mindset. Absorb lessons from those around you, no matter their position—you never know where wisdom may come from.

3. Exceed Expectations

Go above and beyond in everything, no matter how small the task.

Excellence in the small things sets you apart in a world that values mediocrity.

4. Stay Consistent

Faithfulness over time builds trust and opens doors. Establishing a pattern of reliability can be your strongest asset.

5. Guard Your Heart

Protect yourself from frustration, comparison, and pride—distractions that can rob you of the joy in your journey. Remind yourself that success is a process, not a destination.

In All Things

There's a brother in my church, Deacon Phil, who would come in on his off days to serve—filling the baptism pool, cleaning, or preparing communion. I noticed every time he arrived, he stopped at the altar to thank God for the opportunity to serve. Whether taking out trash or preparing for communion, he taught me an important lesson: in all things, give God glory. Every task from God is an honor and opportunity to serve Him.

Reflection

- What small tasks or roles are currently in your life that you might be overlooking? How can you approach them with a mindset of gratitude and purpose?
- In what ways can you demonstrate humility and a willingness to learn from those around you, regardless of their position?
- What steps can you take to exceed expectations in your current role? How will you demonstrate your dedication and work ethic daily?

. . .

Prayer

Father,

Thank You for the opportunities You place before us, even when they seem small or insignificant. Help us embrace each moment with gratitude and humility, knowing that every role is a stepping stone to our purpose.

Teach us to work diligently and with integrity, reflecting Your light in all we do. Guard our hearts against pride and comparison, and give us patience to persevere. May we honor You with our efforts and wait expectantly for the doors You will open.

In Jesus' name, Amen.

7

THE RIGHT POSTURE

In the last chapter, we discussed starting at the bottom of the industry or company to which you are called. But what should you do when your current job looks nothing like the dream God placed in your heart?

When God moved me out of Los Angeles, where I was chasing Hollywood dreams, I found myself working at Enterprise Rent-A-Car. The transition was humbling—going from producing music videos to taking a job I had no passion for, just to make ends meet. At first, I put in the bare minimum, but after seeing I ranked second to last in performance, my competitive nature kicked in.

Within months, I ranked in the top 10 out of 155 employees, earned recognition, and was transferred to an elite branch, where I was groomed for management. I knew this job wasn't my final destination, but it taught me valuable lessons in leadership, customer service, and corporate structure—skills that later became essential in ministry.

When God called me to move from New York City to Lynchburg, Virginia, the transition felt seamless. I transferred to another branch with the same salary, despite the lower cost of living. Looking back, I see how God used that season to prepare me for greater things.

It's easy to feel frustrated when your current season looks nothing like the vision God gave you. But what if this seemingly mundane place is exactly where God needs you? How you handle your current season determines how you'll step into your future.

The Power of Serving in the Now

Joseph's life is a powerful example of serving your current season with excellence. He was a young man with a vision of greatness—a promise from God that one day, even his own family would bow before him.

Yet instead of moving straight from vision to authority, he was betrayed by his brothers, sold into slavery, and later imprisoned. Talk about a disconnect between the promise and the reality.

But Joseph didn't sit and wait for things to get better. He didn't grow bitter or disengaged. Instead, he chose to serve where he was with excellence. Even in prison, Joseph didn't sulk in his pain; he actively served those around him. When the cupbearer and baker were thrown into prison with him, Joseph didn't treat them as lesser people. He used his gift to serve them—interpreting their dreams with wisdom and clarity. By choosing to serve in a place that seemed disconnected from his promise, Joseph positioned himself for his breakthrough.

Joseph didn't misinterpret his situation. He recognized that even in the mundane, God had a purpose. The prison wasn't a place of punishment; it was a bridge—to his promise.

By choosing to serve with excellence, he set the stage for God to elevate him. It was his service, humility, and dedication to excellence in the present that led to his transition from the prison to the palace.

The Hidden Intentions Behind Your Now

It's tempting to believe that where we are now doesn't matter—that it's just a random stop on the way to the "real" destination. We might even feel that our current season is too small or insignificant for God to use. But the truth is, nothing is ever random in God's kingdom. He doesn't waste seasons, and what feels mundane is often part of His intentional process to prepare you for something greater.

Scripture reminds us, "Whoever is faithful in little will also be faithful in much" (Luke 16:10). How we handle the "little" moments shapes us for the larger ones.

When you're faithful in small assignments and seemingly unimportant jobs, you demonstrate to God that He can trust you with more.

Joseph's journey teaches us that our now isn't as random as it may appear. It's part of God's divine strategy. He uses seemingly insignificant moments to refine us, sharpen our skills, and cultivate the character we need to step into our next. What seems like a detour is often God's preparation for your purpose.

A Bridge to Your Promise

Your current season is neither accidental nor random—it is God's preparation ground. No matter how insignificant this season may seem, it is leading you to the next.

Don't overlook small opportunities to serve, and don't grow bitter in the waiting. Instead, embrace this moment as the bridge leading you to your promise.

God is doing something in you right now that will unlock the future He has promised you. Your faithfulness and excellence in this season will open doors and create opportunities beyond anything you can imagine.

Keep your hands to the plow. Keep serving. Keep trusting. And know that your now is a stepping stone, not a stumbling block.

The Right Posture

In the Garden of Gethsemane, at the base of the mountain, Jesus faced an agonizing decision. He was confronted with the choice to embrace a path that weighed heavily on His heart—a path He did not want to walk. Despite being the King of Kings, He chose to humble Himself, adopting the role of a servant. In this moment of deep struggle, He accepted the burden of suffering for the sake of humanity.

Though He had the power to choose otherwise, Jesus willingly embraced servitude, demonstrating profound love and commitment to His mission.

It was this very act of humility and sacrifice in the garden that set the stage for His glorification. As He ascended to the top of Mount Olives, He was revealed not just as a servant but as the King and Savior.

He committed to the challenges before Him in private and was rewarded with a public victory. By maintaining the right posture at the foot of the mountain, God will, in turn, elevate you to the top of it.

Reflection
- Are there any areas in your life right now where you feel stuck or like you're serving in obscurity?
- How can you begin to see your current season as part of God's intentional process for your future?
- What does it look like for you to embrace your now as a bridge to your next?

Prayer
Father,
Thank You for the season I'm in right now. Even when it feels small or insignificant, I trust that You are using it to prepare me for what's next. Help me serve with excellence in this season, knowing that my faithfulness now determines how I step into Your promises.

Help me see You in every moment and serve faithfully in whatever You place before me. I trust You in the waiting and in Your perfect timing, knowing that nothing will be wasted.

In Jesus' name, Amen.

8

HE'S PROTECTING HIS INVESTMENT

I wanted a new pair of headphones, so I went to my local Best Buy.

They had several models on display for customers to try on, test for comfort, and evaluate sound quality.

I sampled a few, comparing the audio quality, weight, and overall experience.

I really wanted to try the Apple AirPods Max, but after scanning the shelves, I realized they weren't available for testing.

Curious, I approached a store representative. *"Hey, where are the new AirPods Max? I don't see them out here. Can I try them?"*

He shook his head.

"Oh no, you can't try those out. The Apple headphones are much more expensive than the others—we protect what we consider valuable. If you want to buy them, I'd have to get the key to unlock them, but you can't test them before purchasing."

That moment spoke to me in a profound way.

The Power of Value and Protection

In life, we often wonder why we aren't as accessible as others, why certain opportunities seem locked away, or why delays happen just when we're eager to move forward. But just like those Apple headphones, God protects what He values.

When something is common, it's easily accessible—anyone can touch it, test it, or walk away from it without a second thought. But when something carries great value, it's placed under lock and key.

It's guarded, reserved, and only released at the right time.

You are not ordinary, and that's why you can't be treated like everyone else.

Some seasons of our lives feel like a waiting room, as if we're tucked away behind glass, watching others be "tested," chosen, or given opportunities.

We wonder why doors seem slow to open, but in reality, God isn't withholding blessings—He is preserving them. He is safeguarding us from being mishandled, under-appreciated, or accessed outside of His divine timing.

Consider Joseph in the Bible. He had dreams of greatness, but God didn't launch him into his purpose overnight.

Instead, he was placed in a 'protective case'—sold into slavery, falsely accused, and imprisoned.

It seemed unfair, but in hindsight, every step was positioning him for elevation. By the time Pharaoh unlocked the door to his destiny, Joseph wasn't just ready—he was fully prepared.

The same is true for us. God holds the key to our lives.

He knows when we're ready to be revealed, when we can handle the weight of our calling, and when it's time for our purpose to be unlocked.

If you feel hidden, overlooked, or delayed, remember: you are not forgotten—you are being protected.

The cost of your calling is too high for God to leave you unguarded.

Temporary Inconveniences for a Permanent Blessing

In the natural, restrictions often feel like limitations. We want things to happen on our timeline, and when they don't, it can be discouraging.

But the key to moving forward with peace and perseverance is understanding that temporary inconveniences often secure a permanent blessing.

Consider a seed—it doesn't sprout into a tree overnight. First, it must be buried, hidden from sight, and endure intense pressure before breaking through the soil. The process may feel uncomfortable, but without it, the seed would never grow into what it was destined to be.

Similarly, when you understand the value of your purpose, calling, and promise, you can endure the process.

Restrictions on time, resources, and personal growth are part of God's divine preparation for what's ahead.

What may feel like a limitation today is often a safeguard for what He's about to bring forth in your life.

The Protection of the Promise

When God gives you a promise, He knows certain things must be refined and developed before you can fully step into it.

Sometimes, that preparation involves waiting, refining, and enduring restrictions that don't make sense in the moment. But these seasons aren't punishment—they are part of God's strategy to protect both you and the promise He has given you.

Think of fish swimming freely in the ocean. While they are free to move within the vast water, even the ocean has boundaries. The shoreline exists to protect the fish—if they cross it, they will die. The boundary provides safety and structure for their existence.

In the same way, God's restrictions in our lives are not meant to hinder us but to preserve us.

Just as a loving parent protects a child from harm, God's boundaries are designed to safeguard what's valuable in us.

Sometimes, the greatest blessing God gives us is His protection while He's preparing us for the promise.

Embrace the Process

Instead of resisting restrictions, we are called to embrace them. When you view them through the lens of purpose, you realize these moments are temporary, but the blessings they prepare you for are permanent.

The inconveniences you face now are helping to secure your future success.

God protects what He values, and what's inside you is too precious to be mishandled or exposed before its time. He is protecting His investment in you.

The longer He preserves you, the greater your harvest will be.

Reflection
- Can you think of a time when a restriction or limitation turned out to be a blessing in disguise?
- What promises has God placed inside of you that are worth the temporary inconvenience of the process?
- How can you shift your perspective to embrace life's, knowing they are part of your preparation?

Prayer

Father,

Thank You for the promise You've placed within me. Help me to see the restrictions in my life not as roadblocks, but as Your protection and preparation for something greater. Give me patience in the process and strength to endure the temporary inconveniences for the sake of the lasting blessing You have for me. I trust that You are shaping, refining, and preparing me for the purpose You've called me to fulfill.

In Jesus' name, Amen.

BE THE BLUEPRINT

I serve as the executive pastor under the greatest preacher in the world—Bishop S.Y. Younger. Call me biased, but I genuinely believe he's the G.O.A.T.—Greatest of All Time.

It is an incredible privilege to serve alongside a world-renowned orator of the Gospel. Bishop Younger preaches God's Word with a unique blend of power, charisma, and Southern humor that resonates with people everywhere.

I also have the honor of serving with Pastor William Westgate, a master communicator of God's truth through modern-day parables—often while rolling on the floor. Regardless of the topic, you can count on Pastor West to end up on the floor and be anointed!

But let's be real: this comes with a lot of pressure. Every time I had the opportunity to preach at Ramp Church International, a wave of anxiety would immediately hit me. People love Bishop's dynamic style and anointing.

Thousands attend our services faithfully, and even more watch online from around the world. They're used to the depth and delivery of a preacher who is a master of his craft.

One day, I shared my struggle with Bishop, confessing how inadequate I felt trying to match his preaching style.

Without hesitation, he looked at me and said, *"When it's your time to preach, that's when God wants to speak through your voice, not mine. Be yourself!"*

That simple, yet profound statement changed everything for me. Anxiety melted away, and I began preaching in my own unique way—with my own style and voice, a touch of New York swagger, and a Hip-Hop flair.

Imitation Kills Innovation

Imitation can stifle innovation. When we focus too much on mirroring what others have done, we often lose sight of the uniqueness God has placed inside us.

God hasn't called you to copy someone else; He's called you to be the blueprint. You are not meant to follow someone else's design but to create something new, something that reflects His purpose for your life.

The truth is, there isn't a blueprint for what God is asking you to do. You're walking a path that has never been traveled before. You are the one who will lay the foundation, shape, and form the vision God has given you.

There are no step-by-step instructions or roadmaps—God has given you a unique assignment that only you can fulfill.

The Danger of Imitation

It's easy to fall into the trap of imitation. We look at successful people and think, If I just do what they did, I'll get the same results. But God hasn't called you to replicate someone else's success.

While there's value in learning from others, your purpose is not to duplicate—it's to create.

Imitating others stifles your creativity and can leave you feeling like a copy rather than a creator. When you're busy trying to be someone else, you miss the opportunity to discover the fullness of what God has designed for you.

You are a masterpiece, designed to bring something new into the world. God hasn't called you to follow someone else's blueprint—He's called you to be the architect of your own.

God's Call to Be the Blueprint

The world doesn't need another version of someone else—it needs *you*. It needs the unique gifts, talents, and perspectives that only you can bring. God has placed within you everything you need to fulfill His calling.

This journey may lead you into unknown territory. There may not be a clear outline for what God is asking you to do, but that doesn't mean you're alone. God promises to guide, direct, and provide for you every step of the way.

At times, It may feel uncertain, but that's part of the adventure. In uncertainty, you have the opportunity to trust Him more deeply and lean on His wisdom as He reveals the beauty of what He's calling you to create.

Innovation Requires Courage

Innovation isn't always easy. It takes courage to forge your path when no clear direction exists. But God is not looking for followers—He's looking for pioneers, trailblazers, and visionaries. He seeks those who are willing to step out in faith and do something different.

Being the blueprint means embracing your individuality and trusting that God's design for your life is far greater than imitation. It takes commitment to your unique vision, even when others may not understand it. And it requires courage to keep moving forward, even when the path isn't clear—knowing that God is with you every step of the way.

The Power of Your Unique Design

When you stop imitating others and start embracing your unique calling, you unlock the door to true innovation. You begin to see possibilities that others don't. You find solutions to problems no one else has considered. You create something entirely new—something only you can introduce to the world.

You are God's masterpiece. He didn't make you to blend in; He made you to stand out. The only way to do that is to stop looking around at what others are doing and start focusing on what He has called you to do.

Release Your Blueprint

God's plan for your life is not a copy; it's an original masterpiece. You are the blueprint for the future He's calling you to create. Don't be afraid to step into the unknown. Don't let fear or comparison hold you back.

Trust that God will guide, equip, and empower you to create something unique—something that reflects His glory.

As you step out in faith to pursue God's calling, remember: the world is waiting for the blueprint only you can provide. Trust God to lead you into uncharted territory and embrace the creative power He's placed within you.

Never forget: God creates but the devil imitates.

As sons and daughters of the Creator, let's walk boldly in our divine inheritance! God is the chief architect, and architects always design using blueprints.

Reflection

- Have imitation or comparison hindered your progress? How can you break free from the pressure to conform?
- What unique gifts, talents, or perspectives has God given you that set you apart? How can you use them to create something new?
- How can you step out in faith and trust God with the unique calling He has placed on your life?

. . .

Prayer

Father,

Thank You for creating me with a unique purpose and calling. You didn't make any mistakes in forming me. You have already accounted for all of my quirks and flaws, yet You still choose to use me for Your glory.

Help me to embrace the blueprint You've given me and to stop comparing myself to others. I trust that You've equipped me with everything I need to fulfill Your will for my life. Give me the courage to step into the unknown and the faith to follow You, especially when the path isn't clear.

I want to be a pioneer, a trailblazer, and a creator—not an imitator. Use me to bring something new into the world for Your glory.

In Jesus' name, Amen.

10

THE BEAUTY THAT PAIN PRODUCED

One of the most impactful lines in *The Five Heartbeats* comes from Duck, who reflects on a reporter's comment: *"You are a truly gifted writer, but you will write your best work when you suffer."*

At first glance, this statement may seem harsh—why should suffering be a prerequisite for greatness? Yet the deeper truth behind these words is undeniable. Struggle refines, shapes, and unlocks depths within us that we never knew existed. Some of the world's greatest works of art, literature, music, and even ministries were birthed in the crucible of suffering.

Consider the Psalms of David—some of his most powerful, soul-stirring writings were penned in caves as he fled for his life. Paul wrote some of his most profound letters while imprisoned. Even Jesus, in His greatest moment of suffering on the cross, fulfilled the most significant act of redemption in history. The pattern is clear: pain often precedes purpose.

The reason suffering produces such deep, meaningful work is that it strips away pretense and forces us to confront our raw, unfiltered selves. It pushes us beyond surface-level thinking and taps into something divine, something eternal. It removes distractions, humbles our pride, and refines our character in a way that prosperity never could.

We often pray for breakthroughs, creativity, and wisdom, yet resist the very process that produces them. We want growth without discomfort, wisdom without experience, and strength without struggle—but it doesn't work that way.

Just as gold is purified through fire and diamonds are formed under pressure, our greatest potential is often unlocked in seasons of difficulty.

The Paradox of Pain and Victory

Throughout history, we see countless examples of individuals who have turned their pain into purpose. Whether it's a preacher delivering a sermon born out of personal trials or an artist crafting their most influential work during periods of emotional turmoil, struggle often births success.

Some of the greatest sermons are preached by those who have walked through deep valleys, endured loss, or fought personal battles. Their words aren't just learned; they are lived—seasoned by real-life experience.

Similarly, many of the most transformative innovations in history have emerged from seemingly hopeless situations. The light bulb, the airplane, and even the iPhone were all products of adversity, trial, and failure.

At one time, each of these inventions seemed like nothing more than a pipe dream—just like the visionaries behind them. Sometimes, it's the closed doors, the denials, and the setbacks that give birth to the most creative and world-changing ideas.

Creativity Born from Pain

The Hebrew word *ke'ev* beautifully illustrates this paradox—it can mean both "pain" and "creativity," highlighting how adversity often births something beautiful.

Just as a diamond is formed under intense pressure, our most creative and transformative ideas can also be birthed through adversity.

God has an amazing way of taking our pain and shaping it into something extraordinary. He uses our struggles not as a deterrent but as a springboard that launches us into greater purpose.

Maya Angelou's poetry was forged in the fire of hardship and injustice. Tyler Perry wrote his first plays while living in his car, turning his pain into a creative force that reshaped his future. None of them would have reached their full potential without the refining fire of adversity.

The Key Is in How We Respond to the Pain

Pain itself is not the end; how we respond to it determines whether it becomes a stepping stone or a stumbling block. How we choose to walk through suffering—leaning into faith, relying on God's strength, and focusing on His purpose—can turn even the most painful experiences into platforms for growth.

When we allow Jesus to work through our pain, He can reveal insights, ideas, and strength we never knew we had.

Embracing the Process of Transformation

As we navigate the highs and lows of life, we must remember that transformation is often not immediate. It requires patience, trust, and the willingness to embrace both the beautiful and painful aspects of life. In every season, there is an opportunity to create something new, to learn, and to grow.

God wastes nothing. Every tear, every loss, and every struggle—He redeems them all for His glory.

Even in the moments when you feel overwhelmed by pain, know that God is working in you. Allow Him to use what seems like a hindrance as the launch pad for your creativity, your dreams, and your purpose.

Like Duck in *The Five Heartbeats*, you may not fully understand why you are going through the struggle, but trust that it's shaping you in ways that will eventually lead to your breakthrough.

The Beautiful Outcome of Pain

If we truly understand the redemptive power of pain, we can begin to view our struggles through different lenses. Creativity, resilience, and innovation often emerge from the most unexpected places—the darkest valleys, the deepest hurts, and the most difficult seasons.

When you find yourself in a season of pain, remember: this is not the end—it's the beginning of something new. Allow God to use your pain as a canvas for creativity, new ideas, and fresh perspectives. In the end, our greatest victories often emerge from our deepest pains. Embrace the process, trusting that God is turning it into something beautiful. Let Jesus work through your pain, and watch as He transforms it into creativity, purpose, and victory.

Reflection

- How have I experienced pain or struggle in my life that later led to growth or creativity?
- Think on a specific moment when hardship led to an opportunity for growth. How did it shape you?
- How can I allow God to use my struggles to fuel my purpose and creativity?

Prayer

Father,

Thank You for the way You redeem our pain and turn it into purpose. Help me to see beyond my struggles and recognize the beauty and creativity that can emerge from them. Teach me to trust the process, knowing You are working—even in the darkest moments.

I pray for the courage to embrace the pain and let You use it for Your glory. May my struggles fuel my creativity, my faith, and my journey toward the purpose You have for me.

Thank You, God, that my pain is not in vain.

In Jesus' name, Amen.

11

MAKE THE CUT

The acclaimed author and preacher, Elder Francine Westgate of The Ramp Church International, once shared that the word "decision" comes from the Latin root *desidere*, meaning "to make a cut."

In other words, our decisions shape our lives—defining what we choose to keep and what we are willing to remove. Pursuing God's will and His purpose requires cutting away anything that stands in the way of His plan.

We often desire to follow God's will and align ourselves with His purpose, yet we fail to realize that saying yes to Him often means saying no to ourselves.

This requires a shift in perspective—a willingness to let go of our plans, desires, and ambitions in exchange for His divine blueprint for our lives.

Though surrender isn't easy, it is essential to walking in the fullness of God's purpose.

The Struggle of Self-Will

We live in a culture that celebrates individuality and self-expression. The pursuit of personal happiness, self-expression, and autonomy is deeply ingrained in us. In this environment, it's easy to believe that our will should always take precedence.

The world tells us we have the right to make our own decisions, follow our preferences, and pursue whatever seems right in our own eyes. We often base our choices on what we want, what we feel, or what seems best in the moment.

However, when we choose to follow Jesus, we are called to live differently. In Luke 9:23, Jesus says, *"If anyone would come after me, let him deny himself, take up his cross daily, and follow me."*

Following Jesus means denying ourselves, laying down our plans, and choosing His will over ours. This is the essence of discipleship: a life of surrender.

The Crossroad of Choices

Each day, we face a crossroads: follow our will or submit to God's. It's a daily decision. Our will often conflicts with God's. Our desires may seem good, but God's plan is always better—even when it doesn't make sense in the moment.

Saying *yes* to God's will acknowledges that His plan is greater than our own. We recognize that He knows what is best for us, even when we don't fully understand it.

Abraham provides a powerful example in Scripture. In Genesis 22, God asks Abraham to sacrifice his promised son, Isaac. Abraham had waited years for this promise, and now God was asking him to surrender it. Yet, in faith, Abraham said *yes* to God, even though it meant saying *no* to his own desires, plans, and understanding. He trusted that God's plan was greater.

Answering God's call often requires letting go of what we thought was best. This can be difficult because our will is often tied to our identity, comfort, or perception of how life should be.

Saying *no* to our will feels like giving up something valuable. But in reality, it is through surrender that God is able to give us something far better than we could ever imagine.

The Reward of Surrender

Surrender isn't about loss—it's about gain. Jesus said in Matthew 16:25, *"For whoever would save his life will lose it, but whoever loses his life for my sake will find it."* The irony of surrender is that it's only in letting go that we find what we were truly searching for.

When we release our own will, we step into the abundant life God has promised. We find fulfillment, peace, and purpose in ways we could never achieve by chasing after our own desires.

Consider the life of Jesus. In the Garden of Gethsemane, just before His crucifixion, He prayed fervently to the Father. He knew the path ahead would be filled with pain and suffering, yet He chose surrender.

In Matthew 26:39, Jesus says, *"My Father, if it is possible, let this cup pass from me; yet not as I will, but as you will."*

Jesus knew that God's will, though painful, was the path to salvation and victory for humanity. He didn't just say *yes* to God's will—He said *no* to His own desire for an easier way.

Because of His surrender, we now have access to eternal life.

Living in God's Will

Living in God's will isn't about perfection or having all the answers; it's about daily surrender and obedience. It's about saying *yes* to God's will, even when it's hard, even when we don't fully understand, and even when it requires us to let go of our own desires.

As we walk in His will, we begin to experience the fruit of our surrender—peace, joy, and a deep sense of fulfillment that only comes when we align with His purpose.

The beauty of surrendering to God's will is that He never asks us to navigate it alone. He walks with us every step of the way, guiding, equipping, and empowering us to fulfill the purpose He has set before us. Saying yes to God means stepping into His best plan for our lives.

Reflection
- What or who might God be calling you to surrender today?
- How can you grow in trusting God's plan, even when you don't understand it?
- In what ways can you actively choose to say yes to God's will and *no* to your own desires?

Prayer
Father,
I surrender my will to You today. I trust that Your plans for me are greater than my own, and I choose to follow You wholeheartedly. Help me to say *yes* to Your will and *no* to my own, knowing that in surrender, I find true life. Thank You for walking with me every step of the way. I trust You with my future and believe that Your plan for me is perfect.
In Jesus' name, Amen.

12

THE HERO TO THE STORY

There's a powerful bond between a father and a child—a bond meant to last, to shape, and to guide throughout life. It's a connection built on trust, love, and the unshakable assurance that, no matter what happens, a good father will always be there.

I remember when I was my daughter's hero—her rock, her safe place, the one she always wanted to be around.

Whether I was watching TV, working on something, or just sitting in silence, she would find a way to be close to me. She would climb into my lap, hold onto my arm, or simply sit beside me, content just to be near her father.

She depended on me for everything—physical, emotional, and even spiritual support. In those moments, I felt like I was her whole world, and truth be told, she was a huge part of mine.

The purity of our relationship, the trust in her eyes, and the way she looked to me for guidance and reassurance made those moments some of the most fulfilling of my life.

But time and life's experiences have a way of reshaping even the strongest bonds.

. . .

The Shift in Our Relationship

As my daughter grew into her teenage years, things began to change. Her world expanded beyond our home, and her attention shifted to friends, school, and new experiences. The father who was once the center of her universe now had to share space with her growing independence.

It wasn't that she loved me any less—no, that love was still there. But the constant need for my presence faded. I watched as she started making her own decisions, forging her own path, and stepping into her identity.

I knew this was natural. It was part of life's progression. After all, isn't this what every parent wants—to raise children who are strong, confident, and capable of standing on their own? And yet, despite knowing this, there was something bittersweet about the transition.

The days when she needed me for everything were fading, and I found myself longing for the times she'd reach for my hand without hesitation.

Then, in a single moment, everything changed.

The Moment of Turbulence

We were on a flight returning from Orlando. It was supposed to be a smooth trip, just another routine flight. But somewhere in the middle of the journey, the plane hit serious turbulence.

I've always been the type of person who can sleep through anything—storms, loud noises, even earthquakes. Turbulence never bothered me— until this time. The aircraft dipped, swerved, and shook violently for what felt like an eternity. The jolts were strong enough to rattle the overhead bins, and I could hear the gasps and nervous murmurs of passengers around me. The sudden jolt woke me, and my first instinct was to check on my daughter. What I saw shattered me.

She was trembling, her eyes filled with tears—fear gripping her as she sat there, uncertain and vulnerable. Without hesitation, I reached over and whispered, *"It's okay. I've got you."* I took her hand in mine, and in that instant, I felt the tension in her body ease just a little. But what moved me most wasn't my reassurance—it was hers.

In that moment, she didn't care about looking strong or independent. She wasn't thinking about her phone, her friends, or anything else. All she wanted was the safety of her father's presence. It was then that I realized something profound—she still needed me.

Maybe not in the same way as when she was a little girl, but the need was still there. And in her most vulnerable moment, when the world around her was shaking, she instinctively reached for the one she knew would protect her.

The Father's Joy

That moment spoke to me on a much deeper level. It made me think about how God must feel when His children reach out to Him in fear, uncertainty, and helplessness. Just as my daughter clung to my hand during the turbulence, we often find ourselves clinging to God when life's storms hit.

The beauty of it is that God doesn't resent our dependence—He delights in it.

So often, we go through life thinking we've outgrown our need for Him. When things are smooth, we loosen our grip. We get caught up in our independence, in our relationships, careers, and ambitions. We don't feel the same urgency to cling to Him.

But then, life happens. A storm hits. The turbulence shakes our world. And suddenly, we realize that the only thing that can bring us peace is the presence of our Father.

I believe God delights when we reach for Him—not just in the hard times but in every season. He longs for us to hold onto Him—not just when the plane is shaking, but even when it's cruising at a comfortable altitude.

Take His Hand Again

After what felt like an eternity, the turbulence finally subsided.

The plane steadied, the tension in the cabin eased, and normalcy returned.

I turned to my daughter and gently teased, *"Do you want me to let go of your hand so you can go back to your phone now?"*

She looked up at me, still holding my hand, and simply said, *"No, I want to keep holding your hand."*

That moment was everything.

Sometimes, after the storm has passed, we realize we don't want to let go.

And maybe—just maybe—that's what the storms are really about.

They aren't meant to break us but to draw us closer—to remind us that we were never meant to walk alone. Maybe God allows turbulence—not to harm us, but to bring us back to dependence on Him. To remind us that His hand has always been there, waiting for us to reach out.

So, take His hand again.

As you pursue your calling, there will be trials and tribulations. There will be turbulence. But every bump on the road, every storm that comes, is another opportunity to grab hold of the Father's hand and find peace in His presence.

Because the truth is—God never lets go.

And He wants to be the Hero in your story.

Reflection

- Are you going through a turbulent season in your life right now? How can you lean on God and allow Him to be your hero in this moment?
- Have there been times when you've let go of God's hand? What steps can you take today to return to Him and hold onto His promises once more?
- How does it feel knowing that God delights in your dependence on Him and your desire to be in His presence?

. . .

Prayer

Father,

Thank You for being my Hero, my Protector, and my Provider. I acknowledge that, in the midst of life's storms, I need Your hand to guide me. Help me never to let go of You, even when I feel strong, because Your strength holds me up. Teach me to trust You fully, to find peace in Your presence, and to hold onto Your hand no matter what comes my way.

In Jesus' name, Amen.

13

THE POWER OF AGREEMENT

A young man serving a long prison sentence seemed perfectly healthy during a routine wellness visit. Yet just days later, he received a devastating diagnosis: he was HIV-positive.

His dreams of reuniting with his family, turning his life around, and finding redemption outside the prison walls were shattered in an instant.

Overwhelmed by hopelessness, his mind and body began to deteriorate rapidly. The once-healthy man lost weight, became frail, and started wasting away before the eyes of his fellow inmates. His posture changed, his energy faded, and his will to fight vanished. Word spread that he was dying, and those around him believed the disease would soon consume him.

Months later, he was called back to the prison doctor's office for a follow-up visit. But instead of discussing treatment options, the doctor revealed something shocking: there had been a mistake. The original test results had been mixed up, and he had never tested positive for HIV. His bloodwork was completely normal.

In disbelief, the man protested as he stared at his frail body. *"Look at me! I'm dying."* Additional tests confirmed there was nothing physically wrong with him. His decline was not caused by an actual disease but by the power of belief. The false report had taken root in his mind, and because he had agreed with it, his body followed suit.

This story is a sobering reminder of the power of agreement. The young man unknowingly made an agreement with a lie, and that agreement shaped his reality. He believed something that wasn't true, and that belief governed his thoughts, actions, and ultimately, his health. But how many times do we do the same thing?

The Lies We Believe and the Power They Hold

Every single day, we are presented with choices about what we will agree with. The enemy constantly whispers lies into our minds, hoping that we will accept them as truth:

- "You're not good enough."
- "Your past disqualifies you from a future."
- "God has forgotten about you."
- "You'll never be free."

And if we're not careful, we start agreeing with those lies. The more we entertain them, the deeper they take root—shaping how we see ourselves, how we see God, and how we walk through life.

The enemy doesn't need to shackle our hands and feet—he just needs to shackle our minds. If he can make us believe a lie, he can make us live it.

But the good news is, just as a false agreement can bring destruction, a true agreement with God's Word can bring freedom.

Agreement with God Brings Life and Victory

The Bible is full of God's truth about who we are:

- "I am fearfully and wonderfully made." (Psalm 139:14)
- "I am more than a conqueror through Christ." (Romans 8:37)
- "He who began a good work in me will complete it." (Philippians 1:6)

Agreeing with God allows His truth to shape our reality. We don't ignore our circumstances, but we choose to believe what God has spoken over us rather than what we see or feel.

In Matthew 18:19, Jesus declares, *"If two of you agree on earth concerning anything that they ask, it will be done for them by My Father in heaven."*

This verse reveals the spiritual law of agreement—what we agree with in our hearts has power. It opens the door for either blessings or bondage, victory or defeat.

What Are You Agreeing With Today?

We see this principle in action in *Numbers 13*, when Moses sent 12 spies to explore the Promised Land.

Ten spies returned with a defeatist report, saying the land was full of giants and impossible to conquer.

But two spies, Joshua and Caleb, came back declaring, *"With God, we are more than able to possess the land!"*

Both groups saw the same land. Both saw the same giants. But their agreement determined their outcome.

- The ten spies agreed with fear—and they never entered the Promised Land.
- Joshua and Caleb agreed with God—and stepped into His promises.

What they agreed with became their reality.

Breaking Free from False Agreements

The young man in prison wasted away because he believed a lie. But what if he had known the truth from the start?

We have the power to break free from false agreements.

- If you've believed the lie that you're unworthy, renounce it and agree with God's truth: You are chosen and loved.
- If you've believed the lie that your past defines you, break that agreement and declare: *"I am new creation in Christ."*
- If you've believed the lie that you will never succeed, replace it with the promise that God's plans for you are good.

Don't accept the false report—reject it!

Final Thought: What Will You Agree With?

The power of agreement is real. It can bring life or death, freedom or captivity, victory or defeat. You don't have to live under false agreements any longer.

Today, choose to align your life with what God says about you. When you do, you will experience the freedom, power, and victory that comes with standing on His Word. Because when you agree with truth, you walk in truth. And when you agree with God, you walk in victory.

Reflection

- Have you ever realized that you were agreeing with a lie from the enemy? How did it affect your life and outlook?
- What are some truths from God's Word that you need to agree with more fully in your life? How can you remind yourself of these truths daily?
- How can you be more intentional about choosing to agree with God's promises, especially during difficult times?

Prayer

Father,

I denounce every lie I have ever come into agreement with. Uproot any falsehoods that I have allowed to take root in me. Thank You for the truth of Your Word that sets me free. Help me recognize enemy's lies and reject them in Jesus' name.

I choose to agree with what You say about me—that I am loved, chosen, and equipped for the purpose You've called me to. No matter the circumstances, I stand firm on Your Word and trust in Your promises. Let Your truth shape my reality today and always.

In Jesus' name, Amen.

14

INTIMACY PRECEDES BIRTHING

I was sitting in a café with my friend and writing partner, Durrel Nelson. We had been collaborating on a script for over a year, carefully crafting every detail. On this particular day, we found ourselves stuck, wrestling with how to introduce a pivotal new character—an elderly woman whose presence would shape the story's direction. We wanted her entrance to feel organic—not forced or cliché—but every idea we came up with fell flat.

After some time, Durrel paused and said, *"Let's pray."*

So we did. We stopped everything, bowed our heads, and offered a simple but powerful prayer, asking God for clarity. No sooner had we said *"Amen"* than an elderly woman walked up to our table. With a kind smile, she asked for help twisting open a bottle cap. I gladly assisted her, exchanged a few pleasantries, and watched as she walked away.

Then it hit me—an "Ah-ha" moment.

I looked at Durrel, and we both knew. That seemingly random moment wasn't random at all. It was an answer. Right there in that café, God had given us the very inspiration we had been searching for. We decided to mirror that real-life encounter in our script, allowing our elderly character to be introduced in an authentic, unexpected way.

It became one of my favorite scenes—one that might never have existed had we not sought God's guidance.

Intimacy Precedes Birthing

This moment reinforced a truth I've come to live by: every great move of God begins in the secret place. Before vision becomes reality and purpose is fulfilled, intimacy must first be established with the One who gives both.

Just as natural birth requires conception, spiritual birthing demands deep, consistent communion with God. Without it, we risk striving in our own strength, relying on human logic rather than divine revelation, and ultimately delaying or distorting what God intends for us.

Too often, we treat prayer as a last resort rather than our first response. But prayer is not just for Sunday mornings or times of crisis—it must be woven into the fabric of our daily lives.

It should be present in the boardroom, the creative studio, the writing process, and every significant decision we face. When we prioritize prayer, we're not just asking God to bless our plans—we're positioning ourselves to receive His plans. And His plans are always higher, greater, and more effective than anything we could come up with on our own.

He reveals hidden things, releases divine strategies, and grants us a prophetic advantage that aligns us with His perfect will. If Durrel and I relied solely on brainstorming and creativity that day, we might still be struggling with that scene.

But because we sought God first, He responded—not with a distant whisper, but with a real-life moment that spoke louder than words.

This is what intimacy with God does. It doesn't just inspire; it guides, directs, and births something greater than we ever imagined.

. . .

Prayer as a Prophetic Advantage

Many people rely on data, experience, and intuition to make business and personal decisions. While these are valuable, they are limited. Prayer, however, gives access to divine wisdom that cannot be attained by human intellect alone.

Through prayer, God grants insight beyond what is visible, giving us supernatural clarity. He leads us to the right people to hire, the right contracts to sign, and the deals to avoid. What seems like a golden opportunity could be a hidden financial disaster—but through prayer, God reveals the unseen.

Think of Daniel, Joseph, and Nehemiah—men who didn't just lead but led through revelation. Their influence was not the result of mere intelligence or ambition but of intimacy with God. Joseph interpreted Pharaoh's dream, positioning Egypt for survival during famine. Daniel sought the Lord and received visions that shaped kingdoms. Nehemiah rebuilt Jerusalem because his heart was burdened in prayer before the work even began.

Each of these men walked in supernatural wisdom because they prioritized intimacy with God.

When we truly grasp the power of prayer, we shift from reactive prayers to preemptive prayers.

We don't just ask for help after making decisions; we seek direction before we ever step forward. This is how we avoid unnecessary delays, heartbreaks, and financial losses.

The Danger of Relying on Human Wisdom Alone

The world teaches us to rely on logic, connections, and experience to succeed. But even the best human wisdom is flawed.

Proverbs 3:5-6 reminds us,

"Trust in the Lord with all your heart and lean not on your own understanding; in all your ways submit to Him, and He will make your paths straight."

Leaning on our own understanding limits us to what is visible. But when we acknowledge God in all our ways, we gain access to divine strategy that transcends earthly limitations. How many business failures, broken relationships, and ministry setbacks could have been avoided if we had sought God's counsel first?

Bringing Prayer into Every Sphere
- **In the Boardroom** – Before making financial decisions, hiring employees, or setting strategic goals, take time to pray. God can reveal whether an investment will bring long-term success or lead to loss.
- **In the Studio** – Creativity is a gift from God, and prayer unlocks divine inspiration. Many worship songs, books, and artistic works are not just crafted but birthed in moments of deep communion with God.
- **In Writing and Planning** – Whether you're drafting a business proposal, a sermon, or a book, invite the Holy Spirit into the process. He can breathe fresh revelation and direction into your work.
- **In Relationships** – Who we align with can shape our future. Prayer gives discernment about partnerships, friendships, and collaborations. Some connections are God-ordained, while others are distractions sent to derail us.

Reflection
- In what areas of your life have you made decisions without seeking God first?
- How can you be more intentional about incorporating prayer into your daily work and decision?
- In what specific areas of your business, ministry, or creative process do you need to surrender control and apply trust in God?

Prayer
Father,
I acknowledge that apart from You, I can do nothing of lasting significance. Teach me to seek You first in every decision I make.

Grant me prophetic insight and divine strategy that align with Your will. Shut doors that are not from You and open those that align with your purpose and plan for my life. Help me to be sensitive to Your voice so that I do not move ahead of You or lag behind. May every endeavor I pursue bring glory to Your name.

In Jesus' name, Amen.

15

ENEMY OF PROGRESS

Distraction is one of the enemy's most lethal weapons. He knows that for many of us, making us doubt God's existence is a lost cause—God has been too real, too present, too faithful. But if the enemy can't make us question God, he'll settle for shifting our focus.

The moment we take our eyes off our divine assignment, we create space for sin to creep in.

The truth is, sin thrives in distraction. However, when we are locked in—laser-focused on the purpose God has placed before us—sin loses its grip. The more we chase after our calling, the less time and energy we have to entertain anything that pulls us away from it.

Idle time is the devil's playground. Just ask King David. When he should have been on the battlefield, he was wandering through the palace. That moment of distraction led him straight to Bathsheba—a decision that nearly wrecked his destiny.

Let's be real—how often have we wasted time, energy, and even money chasing distractions instead of purpose? I know I've been there. I've let people and things pull me away from my assignment.

But no more! I am determined to stay focused. We don't have time to waste—there's too much at stake!

The Power of Focus

When we talk about purpose and assignment, we are referring to the unique calling God has placed on each of our lives. Every believer has an assignment—something specifically designed for them. This assignment is not just a task; it's a calling. It moves us, drives us, and gives us the strength to press forward even in difficult times.

But here's the reality: we can't fully walk in our assignment if we allow ourselves to be distracted by sin. The enemy doesn't always attack with blatant lies or direct doubts about God's character. Sometimes, his most subtle attack is simply distraction—taking our focus off God's plan and redirecting it toward things that don't matter.

In this sense, sin isn't always about outright rebellion against God; sometimes, it's simply about letting our attention drift away from our purpose. When we lose sight of what God has called us to do, we become less effective in fulfilling our calling.

Sin often creeps in when we have idle time—when we aren't actively engaged in what God has called us to do. The more focused we are on our assignment, the less space we have—mentally and emotionally—to entertain sin.

A focused life fills us with purpose and direction, making it harder for distractions—whether sin or otherwise—to take root in our hearts.

Sin as a Distraction

The enemy knows how powerful it is when believers are fully immersed in their God-given purpose. When we're walking in our purpose, we are living out the reason we were created, and that makes us a threat to the kingdom of darkness.

So, what does the enemy do?

He tries to sidetrack us—often with sin. He doesn't need us to outright reject God; he only needs to distract us from the mission at hand.

We see this throughout Scripture.

Hebrews 12:1 reminds us: *"Therefore, since we are surrounded by such a great cloud of witnesses, let us throw off everything that hinders and the sin that so easily entangles, and let us run with perseverance the race marked out for us."*

Notice that sin is described as an obstacle that entangles us. When we're distracted by sin, it's like tripping over our own feet—unable to run the race with the freedom and strength God has given us.

When we focus on the assignment God has given us, the distractions—whether in the form of temptation, sin, or anything else—lose their power.

The more we chase after what God has for us, the less time we have to entertain things that are not of Him.

When our hearts and minds are set on fulfilling our assignment, the pull of sin begins to fade.

What once seemed tempting no longer holds the same appeal.

A Life of Purpose Drowns Out Distractions

The deeper you immerse yourself in God's purpose for your life, the less space distractions have to take hold.

Think about someone deeply engaged in a project that requires their undivided attention. They don't have time to be distracted by irrelevant things. Their mind is focused on the task at hand, and everything else becomes secondary.

Likewise, when you're fully engaged in your divine assignment, sin loses its grip. You become so consumed with pursuing God's call that you no longer have time or energy for the distractions of the enemy.

Your heart and mind are filled with things of eternal value, leaving no room for the fleeting pleasures of sin.

Nehemiah 6:3 says, *"I am doing a great work, and I cannot come down."*

Don't let the enemy's distractions steal your focus or derail your assignment.

. . .

Staying on Course

How do we keep our eyes on the prize and avoid distractions?

1. Set Clear Priorities

Define your assignment and commit to pursuing it. Write it down, speak it out loud, and keep it before your eyes. The clearer your vision, the easier it will be to stay focused.

2. Fill Your Time with Purposeful Activity

Engage in activities that bring you closer to fulfilling your assignment. The more productive and purposeful your time is, the less room there will be for sin to creep in.

3. Stay Close to God

A daily relationship with God through prayer, worship, and studying His Word is the best defense against distractions. The more you know God and His will for your life, the easier it becomes to resist temptations and distractions.

4. Avoid Tempting Situations

If you know certain situations or environments lead you to distractions, avoid them. Guard your heart and mind by staying in places that align with your purpose.

5. Surround Yourself with Like-minded People

Find others who are pursuing God's purpose for their lives. Together, you can encourage each other, hold each other accountable, and make it harder for distractions to take root.

. . .

Reflection
- What distractions in your life have been keeping you from fully focusing on your assignment?
- How can you shift your mindset to prioritize God's purpose over distractions?
- What practical steps can you take today to refocus your energy on fulfilling your assignment?

Prayer
Father,

Help me stay focused on the assignment You've given me. Show me the distractions in my life, and give me the strength to remove anything and anyone that pulls me away from Your purpose. I reject the enemy's attempts to sidetrack me with sin and embrace the fullness of Your calling. Fill me with the passion and perseverance to pursue Your plan, and give me the wisdom to stay on course.

In Jesus' name, Amen.

16

THE WINDS OF PURPOSE

In cross-country running, the headwind is the resistance that feels like it's working against you. It's the force you must push against, the challenge you must overcome, and the burden you must carry.

This wind can be strong enough to slow you down and make each step feel heavier than the last.

Similarly, in life, we often face circumstances that feel like a headwind—a difficult season in marriage, a challenging job, or a personal struggle that seems relentless. The pressure, fatigue, and struggle can feel overwhelming. They can create doubt and make you question whether you're on the right path.

But here's the truth: the headwind doesn't just slow you down—it builds your strength. Facing challenges head-on requires more effort, but with each step, you grow stronger.

You develop resilience, perseverance, and character—qualities essential for fulfilling your purpose. The headwind teaches you to push through adversity and trust that the struggle is an essential part of the process.

Romans 5:3-4: *"Not only so, but we also glory in our sufferings, because we know that suffering produces perseverance; perseverance, character; and character, hope."*

The resistance you face in life is not in vain—it is building something in you that will serve you in the future.

The Tailwind: God's Favor That Propels You Forward

However, there is another kind of wind that is just as powerful in shaping our journey—the tailwind. This is the wind that comes from behind, helping you move faster and further with less effort.

In cross-country running, when the tailwind is strong, it propels a runner forward, giving them a sense of ease in the race. In life, God often sends a tailwind at the right moment. This is His favor, His grace, and His provision carrying you forward when you're in the right position.

It's when things seem to fall into place, when opportunities arise unexpectedly, or when you experience moments of breakthrough that seem to come out of nowhere. These tailwinds serve as reminders that God is with you—leading you, moving on your behalf, and guiding you toward your purpose.

The key is recognizing that both the headwind and the tailwind are part of the same race. The tailwind doesn't eliminate the effort required in the race; it simply accelerates your progress once you've built the strength to move forward.

There are times when God will use His favor to propel you, and other times when He will allow resistance to build your strength. Both are necessary for your growth and success in fulfilling your God-given purpose.

God Is Working All Things for Your Good

Facing a headwind can be discouraging, making us wonder why things aren't moving faster or why we keep encountering obstacles. But if we understand that resistance is part of God's plan, we can shift our perspective.

The struggle is not an indication that we're on the wrong path; it's proof that God is at work, refining us and preparing us for what lies ahead.

Romans 8:28 reminds us: *"And we know that in all things God works for the good of those who love Him, who have been called according to His purpose."*

Both the headwind and tailwind are part of God's divine plan to bring us closer to our destiny.

What feels like a setback is the very thing that propels us toward a breakthrough. God does not waste anything. He uses every circumstance to grow us, teach us, and guide us.

What seems like opposition is the very thing that helps us develop the endurance, wisdom, and character necessary to walk in His purpose.

Embrace the Winds of Your Journey

Whether you find yourself battling against the headwind or enjoying the momentum of the tailwind, trust that God is in control.

Both winds are part of the journey, and each has its purpose.

The headwind builds your strength, and the tailwind accelerates your progress. Together, they move you forward toward the destiny God has prepared for you.

As you navigate the winds of life, remember: God is working all things for your good. Embrace the challenges, knowing they are building your character. Rejoice in the moments of favor, knowing they serve as reminders of God's faithfulness. Trust that in every season, God is working all things together for His glory and your good.

Reflection

- What headwinds are you currently facing? How might God be using this resistance to strengthen you?

- Have you experienced moments of favor or tailwinds in your journey? How can you thank God for those times of grace?
- In what areas of your life can you trust God more fully, knowing that He is working all things for your good?

Prayer

Father,

Thank You for both the headwinds and the tailwinds in my life. I trust that You are using each of them to strengthen me and propel me forward toward my purpose.

Help me to embrace challenges, knowing they build my character, and rejoice in Your favor, knowing it is a sign of Your love.

I surrender my journey to You, knowing that You are always at work, even in the winds that blow against me.

In Jesus' name, Amen.

17

CATCH THE RHYTHM

Some people clap on the 1 and 3, while others clap on the 2 and 4. Then there are those who don't hear the rhythm at all —they clap offbeat, at random, unable to find the cadence.

In any form of music or dance, cadence refers to the rhythm, the flow, and the pacing of the movement. It's the underlying beat that keeps everything in harmony, guiding each note or step in the right direction. Without the right cadence, everything becomes disjointed and lacks the beauty of rhythm.

Similarly, in our walk with God, obedience sets the cadence that keeps us in tune with His purpose, His will, and His timing. When we align ourselves with God's rhythm, we move in harmony with His plans and flow smoothly in the direction He's guiding us.

But when we miss the beat—whether through impatience, distractions, or disobedience—we fall out of sync with His divine timing and purpose.

Just as a song needs its cadence to be beautiful and harmonious, our lives need obedience to stay in sync with God's perfect will. When we are obedient to God, we align ourselves with His divine rhythm. It's a constant flow of listening, responding, and trusting in His direction.

God is always at work in us and through us, and our obedience ensures that we stay in step with His plan, moving according to His divine timing.

Obedience as Alignment

Obedience isn't just about following rules or instructions—It's about aligning ourselves with God's heart and His purpose for our lives.

It's about understanding that God's plan for our lives is far greater than our own understanding, and trusting that His ways are higher than ours. Obedience keeps us aligned with His path, ensuring that we don't wander into places He has not called us to.

When we are obedient, we choose to walk in the cadence that God has established. This means trusting His timing, listening to His voice, and following where He leads—even when it doesn't always make sense or when it's difficult. Obedience keeps us on track, preventing us from wandering into distractions or detours that can delay our progress or take us away from God's will.

Obedience as Trust

Obedience is also a declaration of trust. When we obey God, we are saying, *"I trust You, God, even when I don't understand the full picture."*

Trusting God's direction, even when it seems contrary to our expectations or desires, is an act of faith.

Just as a dancer must trust the choreography or a musician must trust the conductor, we must trust that God knows the way.

His cadence —His perfect rhythm—will always lead us toward His will, even when it seems unclear.

In moments of doubt or confusion, obedience becomes our anchor. It is the commitment to trust in God's plan even when we can't see the entire path laid out before us.

Through obedience, we affirm our belief that God's perfect timing and trust that He is guiding us every step of the way.

The Blessings of Obedience

Staying in cadence with God's will through obedience not only keeps us aligned with His plan, but it also brings about great blessings. Obedience activates God's promises in our lives. When we walk in obedience, we open the door to the blessings He has prepared for us. Just as a musician plays with precision and skill, our obedience brings our lives into harmony with God, allowing His blessings to flow naturally.

God rewards those who obey—not because He's keeping score, but because obedience draws closer to His heart and His plan for our lives. It positions us to receive all that He has for us, both spiritually and practically. When we walk in step with God, we experience His peace, His provision, and His protection.

The Struggle of Obedience

While obedience may seem like the perfect rhythm to follow, there are times when it can be difficult. The world around us pulls us in different directions, tempting us to follow our own desires, to seek comfort, or to ignore the voice of God.

Obedience requires sacrifice—it may mean letting go of our own plans, desires, or comfort to follow to God's leading. It may require patience when we don't see immediate results or understanding. But the struggle is worth it, because obedience ultimately leads us to a place of peace, purpose, and alignment with God's divine will.

The Power of Consistent Obedience

Obedience isn't just a one-time decision; it's a lifestyle. It's the consistent choice to walk in God's cadence every day. Each step of obedience builds upon the last, moving us continuously forward in God's will.

It's through consistent obedience that we experience growth and transformation, becoming more and more aligned with the heart of God.

Just like a song or a dance performance that requires practice and dedication, our obedience is a journey of continual growth and refinement.

The more we obey, the more we attune ourselves to the voice of God, and the more we understand His will for our lives. Consistent obedience keeps us in sync with God's plan and allows His purpose to unfold in our lives.

Stay in the Rhythm

Obedience is the key that keeps us in cadence with God. It is the rhythm that aligns us with His will, teaching us to trust His timing and walk step by step in His direction.

We must stay in tune with God, trusting that His plan is always perfect and His timing is always right. When we choose obedience, we align with God's heart and open the door to His blessings and promises.

Even when the path seems unclear or difficult, let obedience be your guide. Let it keep you on the right cadence, moving in sync with God's will, and trusting that He will lead you to the place of purpose and destiny He has prepared for you. Stay in the rhythm, walk in step with God, and let His will unfold in your life with beauty and grace.

Reflection
- In what areas of your life do you find it difficult to obey God? What is holding you back from trusting His timing?
- How can you actively maintain God's cadence in your daily decisions and actions?
- What blessings or rewards have you experienced when walking in obedience to God's will?

. . .

Prayer

Father,

Help me to stay in the right cadence with You. I want to move when you move. I want to be still when you still. Teach me to trust Your timing and to walk in obedience, even when it's difficult. I want to align myself with Your perfect will, and I believe that You have good things in store for me as I obey. Strengthen my faith and help me walk in rhythm with You every day.

In Jesus' name, Amen.

18

I DON'T LIKE THE WORD PROCESS

About five years ago, I started investing in stocks. I'd heard countless stories of people making millions with the right investments, and I wanted to see if I could join their ranks.

One day, my brother in Christ, Enoch Paku, told me about a stock I should seriously consider. It was priced at $40 per share, and he advised me to buy some.

I followed his advice and made my purchase. Soon after, the stock climbed to $87 a share.

I was feeling pretty good about my decision, but impatience crept in. I decided to cash out early, securing a nice return—but then, the stock soared to $242 a share.

Had I waited just a little longer, my return would have been exponentially greater.

It was a painful lesson, but it emphasized an important truth: patience has value, and the process has power.

The Process: Why Success Takes Time

In a world that thrives on instant results—where fast food and quick access to information are the norm—it's easy to get frustrated when things don't happen as quickly as we'd like. But God's ways are different.

True success isn't born from shortcuts or quick fixes; it is cultivated through a process that requires patience, faith, and the intentional development of strong principles.

"The process takes longer because standards must established before success, and principles before paychecks."

This statement serves as a powerful reminder that lasting success is the result of a deliberate and steady process—one that shapes us into individuals capable of handling both the blessings and responsibilities that come with it. It's not just about enduring the process but also about being prepared to sustain the blessing.

Understanding the Power of the Process

When we go through difficult seasons, we often wonder why things aren't happening faster. Perhaps we're working hard but not seeing the payoff. James 1:3-4 reminds us that the testing of our faith produces perseverance, which leads to maturity. This process of testing and perseverance equips us for greater things.

The process isn't just about taking the right actions; it's about becoming the right person. It's about building standards and principles that ensure we are ready for the success God has in store for us. God is more concerned with shaping our character than putting us in positions of prominence. As we grow in patience and perseverance, we become individuals who can carry the weight of success when it comes.

Building Standards Before Success

Standards are the values that define who we are and how we live. They are non-negotiable values that serve as the foundation for everything we do. Without strong standards, success can be hollow. It might be achieved, but it won't be sustainable.

Just like a house built on a weak foundation won't stand for long, success without solid standards will eventually crumble under pressure.

As we build our standards, we align ourselves with the values of God's Kingdom. These standards shape our behavior, our decisions, and our relationships. They guide us through challenges and help us discern what truly matters. When success comes, we won't bend or compromise because our standards will already be firmly rooted in God's Word.

For example, in your career, it's essential to have standards that govern your relationships, work ethic, and integrity. If you determine never to compromise your values for a paycheck, you will withstand temptation and remain faithful to God's plan for your life.

The process of building these standards may take time, but it's worth it. It creates a life that honors God and sustains long-term success.

Principles Before Paychecks

Principles are the foundational truths that guide our actions. While paychecks and external rewards may be the fruits of our labor, it is principles that sustain us for the long haul.

When we operate based on principles—such as honesty, generosity, hard work, and excellence—we are positioning ourselves for long-term success.

If we are motivated solely by the paycheck, we might lose sight of the greater purpose God has for us. But when we live according to godly principles, paychecks become just one small part of a much larger picture—an opportunity to build God's Kingdom, serve others, and honor Him with our work.

Consider Joseph's story in Genesis. Despite being sold into slavery and facing years of hardship, Joseph held firm to his principles of integrity, faithfulness, and hard work.

His principles guided him through his trials and eventually led him to a position of great influence.

His 'paychecks' came later, but the principles he upheld sustained him.

Trusting God's Timing

The process may take longer than we expect, but it is always in God's perfect timing.

We may not understand why things are taking longer than anticipated, but God is faithful to complete the work He has started in us (Philippians 1:6).

Trusting His timing means recognizing that He is shaping, refining, and preparing us for success that is both meaningful and eternal.

Some aspects of God's purpose can't be rushed. God is looking for those who will endure, those who will abide in Him.

As John 15:4-5 reminds us, "*Remain in me, and I will remain in you... apart from me, you can do nothing.*" Yes, there will be pruning—not to remove you, but to help you bear more fruit.

Don't rush the process. Don't leave the potter's wheel too soon. Every step is molding you to be fit for the Master's use.

Remember, God isn't bound by time—He exists beyond it and can redeem it. He's the same God who extended Solomon's years and held the sun still for Joshua and the Israelites.

Embrace the Process

As you build standards and live by principles, trust that God is at work, preparing you for the success He has in store.

Even when the process feels long and the results seem distant, trust that God is using it for your good and His glory.

He is more concerned with who you are becoming than with the success you are chasing.

Embrace the process.

Allow it to refine, shape, and prepare you for the greater things ahead.

When success comes, you'll be ready to handle it with integrity and wisdom, knowing it was built on a foundation of godly standards and principles that will last.

Reflection
- How can you commit to building strong standards before seeking success?
- In what areas of your life do you need to trust God's timing and process more deeply?
- How do you handle delays or periods of waiting in your pursuit of success?

Prayer

Father,

Thank You for Your faithfulness in shaping me through the process. Help me to trust Your timing and embrace the lessons You are teaching me along the way. Strengthen my character and establish my standards so that when success comes, I can handle it with integrity and wisdom. May my life reflect Your glory, and may I honor You in all that I do.

In Jesus' name, Amen.

19

ARE YOU WILLING TO PUT IN THE WORK?

When we speak of anointing, we often think of divine empowerment—a special grace from God enabling us to fulfill a specific purpose.

It's a gift we cannot earn, yet God gives it to us to carry out His will on earth.

However, there is a common misconception that anointing somehow replaces effort, skill, and preparation. The truth is, anointing is never meant to excuse complacency, laziness, or neglecting the hard work required to master our craft.

In reality, when properly understood, anointing should propel us to work with greater excellence. God's anointing doesn't substitute for diligent practice or the pursuit of mastery—it elevates and empowers our efforts.

The balance between grace and effort, anointing and excellence, is one of the most important lessons we must learn as believers.

The Calling to Excellence

The Bible is clear: God calls us to do everything *"as unto the Lord"* (Colossians 3:23), meaning that whatever gift, talent, or ability He has given us, we are expected to develop it, nurture it, and use it to the best of our ability.

The Apostle Paul compares the life of a believer to that of an athlete striving for a prize. He speaks of discipline, training, and self-control in pursuit of a goal. Athletes don't simply show up and expect to win by divine favor alone; they train rigorously.

Similarly, as someone anointed by God, you are not exempt from the responsibility of honing your skills. Your anointing may open doors and bring favor, but only effort and preparation will sustain you once those doors open.

The anointing might give you a platform, but it's your training and skill that will enable you to lead, create, or minister with impact.

The Example of David

Consider the life of David. God anointed him as king when he was still a young shepherd. That anointing was powerful and set him apart for a divine purpose. But David didn't simply wait for the throne to come to him. He spent years developing the skills necessary to lead, both in the natural and spiritual realms.

As a young shepherd, he learned how to protect his sheep, develop courage, and trust God for victory. Even after his anointing as king, David continued sharpening his military strategy, leadership skills, and knowledge of God's Word.

He didn't rely solely on his anointing; he recognized that God had called him to steward that anointing with excellence. The combination of his God-given gift and his relentless pursuit of mastery is what made David not only anointed, but effective. His preparation was just as important as the anointing.

Anointing Without Effort Leads to Mediocrity

A major danger of misunderstanding the relationship between anointing and excellence is that it can lead to mediocrity. We've all seen gifted people who, believing their natural talent or anointing will carry them, fail to put in the necessary work.

They take shortcuts, neglect training, and rely too heavily on their "gift" instead of developing it. The result? Their impact is often short-lived or less powerful than it could have been.

This is why the Bible encourages us in 2 Peter 1:10 to *"make every effort to confirm your calling and election."* The effort here isn't about earning your calling—it's about being faithful to it through hard work, discipline, and intentionality.

Operating in Excellence

Excellence is not perfection—it's doing the best with what you have. It's being diligent, intentional, and proactive in using your God-given gifts. Excellence is always seeking improvement. It's understanding that every opportunity is a chance to represent God in the best possible light.

As you operate in excellence, remember that your work, whether in ministry or in the marketplace, speaks volumes about your relationship with God. People may not always recognize the anointing on your life immediately, but they will notice your excellence. They will see the dedication, passion, and consistency you bring to your work. And that excellence becomes a testimony of God's goodness and faithfulness in your life.

Anointing is Not an Excuse for Laziness

Anointing is not an excuse for lack of preparation. It's doesn't bypass strategic planning, justify unprofessionalism, or excuse carelessness. You are not the only one anointed—don't expect the world to cater to you.

Anointing doesn't mean you just show up and let God do everything for you. Don't use God as an excuse to be lazy or unprepared.

God can work in any situation, but He won't elevate you to a place you're not prepared for, nor will He won't bring shame to His name.

The same God who moved in your chaos because of His grace can move even more powerfully when you partner with Him in preparation and excellence. Because you represent God's Kingdom, you should strive to be even more diligent, professional, and efficient.

God is excellent in all His ways, and we are called to reflect His nature in everything we do.

Anointed for Excellence

Your anointing is a powerful gift, but it also carries a responsibility. It is a grace that calls you to a higher standard—one that doesn't allow you to sit idly by while others labor. Instead, it empowers you to put in the work necessary to bring glory to God through your gifts.

God has given you a unique purpose, and He has anointed you for it. But anointing without effort leads to stagnation. Anointing with excellence, however, leads to transformation—not just in your life, but in the lives of those around you.

Don't allow the gift of anointing to become an excuse for laziness. Instead, embrace it as the catalyst to pursue excellence, sharpen your skills, and fulfill your calling with all your heart, mind, and strength.

God is waiting for you to do your part. As you do, His anointing will make your efforts fruitful, elevating your work beyond what you could achieve on your own.

The Difference Between Anointing and Effort

I used to play basketball at *The Cage*, the famous court on West 4th Street in the Village, where trash talk was always at an all-time high.

One day, an older guy on the court claimed he could have been better than Michael Jordan—after all, he was naturally tall, athletic, and skilled.

But the guy defending him responded with raw honesty:

"You could have been—but your laziness was your impediment. The difference between you and Mike? He was willing to put in the work."

Talent alone is not enough. Anointing is the gift—but effort is the investment. Talent is potential, but discipline unlocks it. Favor may open doors, but only preparation will keep you in the room.

Just like Michael Jordan wasn't simply born great—he became great through relentless practice, sacrifice, and commitment—our anointing requires effort to reach its full potential.

The question isn't just whether you're anointed—the question is, are you willing to put in the work?

Reflection
- How do you currently view the relationship between God's anointing and the effort you put into your work or calling?
- Are there areas in your life where you have been relying too much on your anointing and neglecting the need for preparation and effort?
- What practical steps can you take to pursue excellence in your God-given assignments?

Prayer
Father,

Thank You for the anointing You have placed on my life. I recognize that this gift is a powerful tool to fulfill Your purpose, but I also know it requires responsibility and effort. Help me never to use Your anointing as an excuse for laziness or complacency.

Teach me to steward my gifts with excellence, to develop my skills, and to put in the work necessary to fulfill the calling You've placed on my life. Empower me by Your Spirit to pursue excellence in everything I do, that through my efforts, Your glory may be revealed to the world.

In Jesus' name, Amen.

20

THE 4TH WATCH CREW

The night before I preach, I prioritize going to bed early—not just to rest, but for preparation. I know that what happens in the early hours of the morning will shape everything that follows.

At 4 a.m., before the world stirs and the noise of the day begins, I rise—not out of habit, but by necessity. This is the sacred hour when I hear God most clearly. Even after weeks of studying, meditating, and meticulously outlining my sermon, the message never fully takes shape until those pre-dawn moments.

It's in the stillness, when everything is hushed and undisturbed, that I feel the weight of His presence most profoundly. In that solitude, distractions fade, revelation flows, and the Word moves from my mind to my spirit.

That early morning communion is more than just the final step in preparation—it is an encounter. It's where God refines, redirects, and breathes fresh life into what He has already placed in my heart.

Waking Early: A Strategic Advantage

Rising before dawn isn't merely an act of discipline—it's a strategic advantage. While the rest of the world sleeps, I step into a realm where distractions are silenced, and destiny takes shape.

In that sacred solitude, my focus sharpens, my heart aligns, and I gain a divine perspective on the assignment ahead.

More than just a routine, this morning encounter is a moment of alignment and empowerment.

By the time the world awakens, I have already been in the presence of the Almighty. I've received clarity, fresh revelation, and a renewed fire.

My day doesn't start with uncertainty—it begins in victory.

The Fourth Watch: A Sacred Window

The fourth watch of the night, traditionally from 3:00 AM to 6:00 AM, carries deep spiritual significance.

This time has long been recognized as a sacred window for divine connection and supernatural breakthrough.

In scripture, Jesus often withdrew to pray during these hours. Matthew 14:25 recounts that during the fourth watch, He walked on water toward His disciples, demonstrating both His power and His deep communion with the Father.

For many believers, this time serves as a spiritual threshold—a moment when heaven seems near, clarity is heightened, and divine wisdom is more readily received.

It is in these quiet hours, before the world stirs awake, that we can pour out our hearts to God without distraction and prepare our spirits for the challenges ahead.

The Power of Starting Early

Beyond the spiritual realm, the principle of rising early is embraced by many successful individuals across various fields. Leaders, entrepreneurs, and athletes often attribute their achievements to the discipline of beginning their day before the rest of the world wakes. The stillness of the morning provides an opportunity to focus, plan, and set intentions without the interruptions of daily responsibilities.

Psalm 5:3 reminds us: *"In the morning, Lord, You hear my voice; in the morning I lay my requests before You and wait expectantly."*

By dedicating our mornings to prayer, reflection, and focus, we not only set the trajectory of our day but also align ourselves with God's will and purpose. The morning hours become a time of strategy, impartation, and preparation—both spiritually and practically.

Building Your Morning Routine

The fourth watch offers a unique window for spiritual growth and divine connection. However, the principle of starting your day with purpose remains relevant, regardless of when you wake up. The key is to dedicate the beginning of your day to what matters most—seeking God, aligning your priorities, and preparing yourself mentally, physically, and spiritually for the day ahead. A well-structured morning routine can set the tone for a day filled with clarity, productivity, and spiritual alignment.

1. Start with Prayer and Worship

Begin your day by engaging with God. This sacred time allows you to surrender your plans, express gratitude, and seek divine wisdom. Whether by reading Scripture or simply sitting in His presence, dedicating your first moments to God helps align you with His will.

2. Tackle the Hard Tasks First

The early hours provide uninterrupted time for deep focus, making them ideal for tackling your most important or challenging tasks. Whether for strategic planning or creative work, dedicating this time to high-priority tasks helps you operate with intention.

. . .

3. Plan Your Day with Purpose

Rather than moving through the day reactively, take time to set clear intentions. When we allow God's priorities to shape our day, we become more effective and intentional with our time.

4. Care for Your Body and Mind

Our spiritual well-being is intricately linked to our physical and mental health. When we steward our bodies well, we cultivate the strength, energy, and focus needed to walk fully in our calling. So get up, get moving, and take care of the vessel God has given you!

The Intersection of Spirituality and Productivity

There is a profound connection between spiritual discipline and practical success. The world often promotes morning routines for increased efficiency, but for believers, mornings aren't just about productivity—they're about divine alignment.

By dedicating the first moments of the day to God, we receive fresh revelation, wisdom, and strength to navigate our responsibilities with clarity and peace. Many of history's great leaders, both spiritual and secular, have credited early mornings for their effectiveness.

But as believers, our goal isn't just success—it's walking in step with God's purpose. Whether you embrace the fourth watch or create a personalized morning rhythm, prioritizing God and meaningful work in the early hours will transform your life.

So, as the world says, *"The early bird catches the worm."*

But for us, it's not just about seizing opportunities—it's about receiving divine revelation, wisdom, and strength for the journey ahead.

Reflection Questions

- When was the last time you dedicated quiet time with God in the early morning? How did it impact your day?

- What are the biggest obstacles preventing you from waking up early or starting your day with purpose?
- How can you restructure your mornings to cultivate both spiritual and practical growth?

Prayer

Father,

Thank You for the gift of a new day. As I rise each morning, meet me in the quietness of the early hours. Let my first moments be filled with Your presence, drawing me closer to You and aligning my heart with Your will. Grant me the discipline to seek You first, handle my responsibilities with wisdom, and embrace each day with faith and purpose.

May my mornings be a sacred space for renewal, insight, and divine strategy. I surrender my plans, my work, and my heart to You. Be glorified in all I do today.

In Jesus' name, Amen.

21

YOU CAN'T ESCAPE IT

It was Sunday morning, July 8, 2021. I arrived at the church about an hour and a half before service—my usual routine. But this morning felt different.

I had just returned from Montego Bay, Jamaica, with my wife.

As I walked down the hallway to my office, my mind drifted back to those peaceful days by the ocean—days when I wasn't carrying the weight of responsibility, when for once, I was just Marvin, not Pastor Marvin.

As quickly as the memories came, so did the reality check—ministry was waiting for me on the other side of that hallway. And I was tired.

Tired of pouring out.

Tired of meeting people's demands.

Tired of carrying the weight of leadership and the never-ending church drama.

I love my church. I love what I do. But, it was becoming too much.

I never asked for this. Pastoring was never my dream. I missed the freedom of just being Marvin. And that morning, as I walked into service, I asked myself, *Do I still want to do this?*

I put on the Sunday smile, shook hands, and went through the motions. But inside, I was wrestling.

Then came the sermon.

Bishop S.Y. Younger took the mic and after reading the Scripture, he said, *"Before you take your seat, look at your neighbor and ask them, Neighbor, do you still want to do this?"* And just like that, Jesus got all in my business.

In that moment, I knew—God saw me. He heard the silent cries I hadn't spoken. He understood exactly where I was. But here's the thing: He didn't hand me an escape route. He didn't give me permission to walk away. Instead, He reminded me: *You still have to do what I called you to do.*

God never consulted me about His idea for my life. He chose it for me. And like Bishop always says, *"You can catch your breath, but you don't get to quit."*

You Can't Outpace God's Calling

There is something profound about God's calling on our lives. No matter how far we run, how many times we quit, or how many detours we take, the calling remains—unchanged and irrevocable.

When God has ordained a purpose for you, it stands firm. You can try to ignore it, bury it, or convince yourself it isn't there, but the truth is, you can never outrun what God has set in motion. At best, you may delay it—but even then, His purpose will always find its way back to you.

We think we can outrun it, believing that if we get far away, it will fade into the distance. But the more we run, the closer we get to the truth that we can't escape it.

The Runaway Prophet: Jonah's Story

Jonah's story is a powerful example of resisting God's call. When God sent him to Nineveh, Jonah fled in the opposite direction, boarding a ship to Tarshish to escape. But God sent a storm, forcing him to confront his calling. Swallowed by a great fish, Jonah spent three days in reflection, wrestling with his rebellion. Once released, he obeyed, leading to a great revival in Nineveh. Despite his resistance, Jonah couldn't escape God's unshakable purpose.

Running in Circles

How often do we run from God's call, trying to outrun the sense of purpose He has placed in our hearts? We take detours, make excuses, or tell ourselves that we're not ready yet. We may even quit—maybe not physically, but we quit in our minds. What we fail to realize is that we can't outrun God's plan.

It's a painful, frustrating process because deep down, we know we are only delaying the inevitable. We may waste years—or even decades—fighting against our purpose, but eventually, God will bring us right back to the very place we've been avoiding.

God has a script for your life. You can choose to play your part, or you can try to rewrite the script. But no matter how many edits you make or how many scenes you skip, you can't change the ending. Your calling will always come for you, and it will always pull you back to the path you're meant to walk.

You Can't Quit What's in Your Blood

It's easy to think that you can quit—mentally or physically—when the pressure of fulfilling your purpose becomes too great. But the reality is, you can't quit what is in your very DNA. God has placed this purpose inside of you, and it's not something you can escape, no matter how much you may want to.

In fact, you'll find that the more you try to quit, the more unsettled you'll become. Your heart will feel restless, your spirit uneasy, because the calling of God is irrevocable. It's like trying to run from a part of yourself. It's in your blood. It's in your bones. It's who you are. And no matter how long you run, at some point, you'll realize that it's time to step into it.

Get With the Program

The quicker we accept that God's purpose for our lives is non-negotiable, the quicker we can walk in peace and purpose. The longer we fight against it, the longer we delay the joy, fulfillment, and growth that comes from walking in our calling.

There's freedom in surrender. When you finally submit to God's plan, you open the door to the life you've been searching for all along. The life of peace that makes sense because it aligns with the divine purpose for which you were created.

Get with the program. Stop wasting time trying to outrun what God has already ordained for you. The sooner you accept His call, the sooner you'll can walk into the fullness of what He has for you. Don't waste another moment running in circles. Step into your purpose and let God use you in the mighty way He's always intended.

Conclusion: Submission Brings Freedom

The calling on your life isn't something you can escape, and it's not something that will ever fade away. You might try to run, you might quit in your mind, but God's purpose for you is unwavering.

You can either embrace it now and walk in the freedom of submission, or you can resist and delay the inevitable. But at the end of the day, God's purpose will prevail. Stop wasting time trying to outrun what God has already ordained for you. You're called for greatness and purpose. And that calling will always find its way back to you, no matter how many detours you take.

Submit to it. Trust in it. Walk in it. And watch as God uses your life in ways you never imagined.

Reflection

- Are there areas in your life where you've been running from God's call?

- What would it look like if you fully embraced the calling on your life today?
- How can you take the first step toward surrendering to God's purpose for you right now?

Prayer

Father,

Thank You for the calling You have placed on my life. I confess that there are times when I've tried to run from it, or when I've convinced myself that I'm not ready. But today, I choose to surrender to Your will. Help me to stop running, embrace Your plan with faith, and to walk in the fullness of my calling. I know that in surrendering, I find peace, purpose, and the life You have always intended for me.

In Jesus' name, Amen.

22

IS IT TO GOOD TO BE TRUE?

Have you ever heard the phrase, *"If it sounds too good to be true, it probably is"*? It's a mindset many of us carry, often as a way to protect ourselves. This belief stems from caution, past hurt, and disappointment. It's the voice in your head that says, *"Don't trust that opportunity. Don't believe that person. Don't allow yourself hope too much—it might fall apart, just like everything else in your life has."*

While this mindset may serve as a protective barrier, it can also limit us from walking fully into the promises God has for us. This skepticism doesn't just affect how we view people or opportunities; it also shapes how we view God's blessings.

Fear of disappointment, coupled with the scars of past letdowns, can keep us from fully embracing the good things God has for us. Worst of all, it traps us in a cycle of doubt, preventing us from stepping into the freedom He's already provided.

I've spoken to many people who struggle to accept anything that sounds "too good to be true," especially when their past is filled with disappointment or betrayal.

I recently talked with a young man who was skeptical of a simple process I shared with him to rebuild his credit. *"That sounds too good to be true,"* he said, shaking his head in disbelief. His past struggles had made him suspicious of any good opportunity, fearing it would turn into another disappointment. This isn't just a financial struggle—it's a spiritual battle.

Why Do We Believe It's Too Good to Be True?

Trauma leaves lasting marks on the heart and mind. For some of us, growing up in environments where trust was broken—whether by family, friends, or the system itself—creates patterns of fear and suspicion.

People who were supposed to protect us turned on us. Friends betrayed us. Systems that should have helped us exploited us. We were misled, scammed, or left behind in a world that promised safety but delivered harm.

Over time, these experiences distort our ability to see the goodness in others—and more importantly, to see the goodness of God. We carry a lens of suspicion that tells us, *"If it sounds too good to be true, it's probably not real."* And that lens can keep us from accepting the truth of God's promises.

We begin to convince ourselves that His blessings, too, are too good to be true—just like the deceptive offers we've encountered in the world.

But here's the truth: God's goodness is not a scam. It's not too good to be true—it's exactly what He promised.

The Truth About God's Goodness

The Bible is full of promises about God's goodness, and we need to remember them every day. In Romans 8:32, we read, *"He who did not spare His own Son, but gave Him up for us all, how will He not also, along with Him, graciously give us all things?"*

Let that sink in for a moment. God gave His very best for us—so why would He withhold anything good?

When we believe that God's blessings are *"too good to be true,"* we are rejecting His promises. Why? Because we have allowed past disappointments to dictate how we view His character. But God's nature is to bless. His desire is to do immeasurably more than we could ask or imagine. That's His heart toward us!

God is not a trickster. The good things that come our way—whether they are opportunities, relationships, or grace—are gifts from a good God.

Faith in God, Not in the System

Here's where we need to draw a crucial distinction: We are not placing our faith in the systems or people themselves, but in God, the One who can use them to bring us into our promised place.

We don't put blind trust in the stock market, job systems, or human relationships blindly. We trust God's ability to use them to fulfill His will.

God can work through the systems and people in our world—even those we sometimes doubt or fear. Whether it's a job opportunity, a financial breakthrough, or a new relationship, He can use them to accomplish His purposes for our lives. But we must let go of the limiting belief that good things are always too good to be true. Instead, we must trust that God is in control of everything, even when things look too good to be true through our eyes.

The Invisible Chains of Shame

This mindset doesn't just affect how we view opportunities; it also impacts how we view ourselves. If we can't embrace the good things that God has for us because we are still stuck in shame or guilt, we will never fully walk in His freedom.

The invisible chains of shame and condemnation bind us in a prison of self-doubt and fear. We rehearse our past mistakes, failures, and shortcomings, convincing ourselves that God could never forgive us completely.

But here's the truth: The chains don't exist. They've been broken. Colossians 2:13-14 says, *"When you were dead in your sins... God made you alive with Christ. He forgave us all our sins, having canceled the charge of our legal indebtedness, which stood against us and condemned us; He has taken it away, nailing it to the cross."*

God has already freed us from the weight of our past, so we no longer need to live under shame's burden.

If we continue to believe we are still chained to our past mistakes, we won't be able to accept the blessings God has for us today. But when we understand that we've been forgiven and that the chains are gone, we can step forward into His plan with confidence, knowing that He has already taken care of everything that once held us back.

Embracing God's Grace and Forgiveness

God's grace is abundant. His forgiveness is complete. His blessings are real. He has called you to something good—something extraordinary yet perfectly aligned with His love for you. If you've been living in the shadow of past trauma or doubt, or if shame has blocked your path, I encourage you today to embrace His grace.

Trust Him. Trust that He is a good Father who desires the best for you, and that He will lead you into your promised place. The chains of doubt, shame, and fear have no hold on you anymore. You are free. You are forgiven. And God's good plans for your life are waiting for you to step into them.

Don't let the past hold you back. Embrace the good things God has for you—because they're not too good to be true. They're exactly what He wants for you.

Reflection

- Are there areas in your life where you've been hesitant to trust God's goodness, believing it's "too good to be true"?
- How has past trauma or disappointment shaped the way you view God's promises?
- What is one blessing or opportunity you've hesitated to embrace because it seemed too good to be true?

Prayer

Father,

Help me to release the skepticism that has kept me from fully embracing Your blessings. I surrender my doubts, my fears, and my past disappointments to You. Thank You for Your goodness, which is not too good to be true, but exactly what You have promised. Today, I choose to trust You more deeply and step boldly into the future You've prepared for me.

In Jesus' name, Amen.

23

PIVOT

New York University was my dream school. Many of my film heroes—Spike Lee, Mahershala Ali, Billy Crystal, and Jeffrey Wright—had studied there, and my oldest sister had also attended.

Located in the vibrant Greenwich Village neighborhood of Manhattan, NYU felt like the perfect place for me. I spent countless hours on campus—participating in fashion shows, befriending older students, and truly feeling like I belonged. I believed it was my destiny.

Confident in my grades, extracurriculars, and faith, I applied for early admission. I prayed and trusted God. But when the letter arrived, it began with,*"We regret to inform you..."*

My heart sank. I was devastated and even considered not going to college at all.

Then, out of nowhere, a pamphlet from Fordham University arrived in the mail. I didn't know much about Fordham, but as I flipped through it, I noticed their acting program and learned that Denzel Washington was an alumnus. That sparked some hope, so I applied. When the acceptance letter arrived, I realized this wasn't my original plan, but it might be God's.

At Fordham, I met Eric Johnson, my academic advisor, who became a pivotal figure in my life. He introduced me to Norman Augenblick, one of his former students, who interviewed me for an internship at Sean "Diddy" Combs' executive office.

That internship opened the door to two incredible years of invaluable experience. From there, I worked with film producer Connie Orlando, who later became Vice President and Head of Programming at BET Networks.

This experience ultimately opened the door for me to become an assistant to Hype Williams, one of the greatest music video directors of all time. None of this would've happened if I hadn't pivoted after NYU's rejection.

What seemed like a setback was God's way of rerouting me to opportunities that shaped my journey and ultimately led me to the same destination.

What Do You Do When God Closes a Door?

What do you do when you come to a crossroads or face a closed door? What do you do when you're pursuing God's will, and the path you thought would lead to your purpose suddenly shifts? Do you retreat? Do you give up? Do you abandon everything you've worked for, or do you pivot?

Pursuing your purpose is a journey, not a straight line. Along the way, you'll encounter moments when the path is unclear, when your efforts don't yield the results you expected, or when the direction you thought was right suddenly feels off-course.

It's in those moments that the ability to pivot—to shift direction—becomes essential.

In basketball, pivoting is a fundamental move. A player keeps one foot grounded while using the other to shift direction. This simple move isn't a sign of failure—it's about maintaining balance, flexibility, and adaptability.

In much the same way, pivoting in your purpose is not about

giving up—it's about growth, resilience, and the ability to adapt when God calls you to shift.

The Power of Pivoting

Sometimes, we become so focused on a specific goal or vision that we become rigid. We tell ourselves, *"This is the way it's supposed to happen,"* but purpose is rarely a straight path. More often , it's winding —requiring us to adjust and realign as God reveals His plan.

Pivoting isn't failure; it's learning to trust God's wisdom and timing instead of clinging to your own limited understanding. When you pivot, you acknowledge that the direction you once thought was right might not be the best one after all—and that's okay.

It doesn't mean you've failed; it means you're listening, adjusting, and staying aligned with God's leading.

In fact, pivoting can lead you to a greater purpose than you ever imagined. It keeps you moving forward. You're not stuck; you're adapting to the changing circumstances and still pressing toward the higher call on your life.

Faith to Pivot: A Lesson from Paul's Journey

In Acts 16, Paul was faithfully carrying out God's call. He risked his life—traveling day and night, pouring everything he had into spreading the gospel. But when he reached Asia Minor, the Holy Spirit forbade him from preaching there. He tried to go south, but again, God shut that door.

Ever wondered why God shuts a door on what seems like a good opportunity? It doesn't make sense. But Paul didn't quit. Instead, he pivoted and went to Macedonia.

It was in Macedonia that Lydia was baptized. It was there that a slave girl was delivered. It was in Macedonia that Paul planted churches in Philippi, Thessalonica, and Corinth—the very churches to which we owe five of the New Testament epistles. Because Paul's faith led him to pivot, the gospel spread to Europe, opening the doors for Christianity to reach generations across the continent.

Faith isn't afraid to pivot; it's afraid of not pivoting.

Could it be that the reason God closed a door in your life is because He has a greater one waiting for you—a door that will impact future generations?

What's incredible is that, later on, God opened the doors in Asia Minor for Paul to do the work he originally intended. But God's plan was bigger and more eternal than Paul could have imagined.

The Strength in Flexibility

We live in a world that often rewards rigidity. We're told to stay the course, no matter what. But in the kingdom of God, flexibility is a strength.

Just like a tree's roots grow deeper when it faces the wind, your purpose grows stronger when you learn to adapt.

Pivoting opens the door to new opportunities, untapped potential, and a deeper relationship with God. It shows that your trust in His plan is stronger than your attachment to a specific outcome.

In your pursuit of purpose, be willing to pivot. Don't be afraid to make changes when it's clear God is leading you in a new direction.

Pivoting doesn't mean failure—it's part of the process of becoming who God has called you to be.

Reflection

- Think of a time when you had to pivot. How did it open new doors?
- What does it mean to you to remain flexible in your pursuit of God's plan for your life?
- How can you trust God more deeply when it feels like a pivot is required?

. . .

Prayer

Father,

Help me trust in Your guidance and timing, especially when I feel uncertain about the direction I'm headed. Give me the strength to pivot when needed, knowing it's not failure but a step closer to Your purpose. Help me to remain flexible and open to the changes You bring, and to trust that each pivot brings me closer to the calling You've placed on my life. Your plan is perfect. I trust You.

In Jesus' name, Amen.

24

ONE THING

My good friend Elder Kelly Galloway, once shared a dream she had about me—one that left me uneasy at first. In the dream, I stood beside a brick house, pressing against different bricks, but nothing happened.

Brick after brick, I pushed, searched, and struggled—until I found the right one.

The moment I touched it, the entire structure collapsed over me. I remember telling her, *"I don't think I like this dream."*

But then she smiled and said, *"Those bricks didn't fall to crush you— they fell to bless you."* They represented opportunities, breakthroughs, and favor.

The key wasn't pushing everything at once—it was applying pressure to the right one. The one that would set off a chain reaction of abundance.

Sometimes, it's not about working harder—it's about discerning where to apply the pressure.

Focus on One Thing

In a world full of distractions and endless opportunities, many of us feel pulled in multiple directions. If you're multi-talented or have big dreams, it's easy to try to doing everything at once. The problem with this approach is that it often leads to busyness without progress —activity without productivity.

God has given each of us unique talents, gifts, and dreams, but He is also a God of strategy, wisdom, and execution. As 1 Corinthians 14:33 reminds us, *"For God is not a God of confusion but of peace."* He calls us to walk in order, not chaos, and sometimes that means putting complete focus on one thing at a time.

The Problem with Spreading Yourself Too Thin

Jeff Bezos started Amazon in 1994 as an online bookstore. He had great visions for Amazon taking over multiple industries, but he first focused on the online book market.

Once he mastered that area, he expanded into other sectors like electronics, clothing, and film—and eventually became a global marketplace.

Bezos's journey shows the power of mastering one thing before expanding. By building a strong foundation, he created opportunities to explore new ventures successfully.

This principle applies to any goal—focus, discipline, and execution in one area can unlock doors to greater possibilities.

When you try to juggle too many tasks or projects simultaneously, your energy and attention become divided. Imagine working on five projects at once—if you're giving 20% of yourself to each, then none of them is receiving your full potential. Instead of excellence, you may end up with mediocrity.

While multitasking has its place, there's a difference between managing small tasks simultaneously and trying to accomplish multiple significant goals at once.

Major accomplishments require focus, dedication, and effort— none of which can happen when you're stretched too thin.

. . .

God Is a God of Strategy

Throughout Scripture, we see examples of God's strategic nature.

He didn't simply give Moses the vision for the tabernacle; He gave specific instructions for its construction.

When Nehemiah rebuilt the walls of Jerusalem, he didn't rush into the work blindly; he inspected the walls, developed a plan, and led the people with clarity and focus.

Similarly, God has a strategy for your life. But His plans require your obedience and focus.

When He gives you a vision or idea, it's not just about starting—it's about finishing.

2 Corinthians 8:11 urges us: *"Now finish the work, so that your eager willingness to do it may be matched by your completion of it."*

Something powerful happens when you complete a work.

It brings honor to God, builds confidence in you, and prepares you for the next level.

Unlocking Doors Through Focus

Many of us are waiting for God to open new doors, but He's waiting for us to finish the first assignment. Why would He trust us with more if we haven't completed what He's already asked us to do?

When you focus on one thing and bring it to completion, it can unlock other opportunities. That one door often leads to many others —but first, you must identify the *"one thing"* God wants you to focus on in this season.

Practical Steps to Focus on One Thing

1. Identify Your "One Thing"

Pray and ask God to reveal the area where He wants you to focus. This might be a specific project, relationship, or area of personal growth.

2. Set Clear Goals

Once you know your "one thing," break it down into actionable steps. Clear goals keep you on track and give you a sense of progress.

3. Eliminate Distractions

Identify what pulls your attention away from your goal. Whether it's social media, unnecessary commitments, or procrastination, take steps to limit those distractions.

4. Commit to Completion

Discipline yourself to stick with the task until it's finished. Remember, starting is easy; finishing is where the growth happens.

5. Trust God's Timing

Just because you're focusing on one thing doesn't mean your other dreams are forgotten. Trust that when the time is right, God will open the door for the next thing.

A Biblical Reminder

Think about Jesus during His earthly ministry. He was clear about His purpose: to do the will of His Father. Even with crowds, demands, and distractions, Jesus remained focused. He didn't rush or try to do everything at once. He moved with intentionality, completing the work He was sent to do. If Jesus, the Son of God, operated with focus and purpose, how much more should we?

Reflection

- What is the "one thing" God is calling you to focus on?

- Have you been spreading yourself too thin by trying to juggle too many projects or responsibilities?
- What steps can you take to eliminate distractions and finish what God has called you to do?

Prayer

Father,

Thank You for being a God of strategy, wisdom, and order. Help me focus on the assignment You've given me in this season. Show me the "one thing" You want me to pursue and give me the discipline to stay committed until it's finished. I trust that as I honor You through my obedience and focus, You will open new doors and guide me into the next steps of my purpose. I just want to do your will.

In Jesus' name, Amen.

25

BUILD UP YOUR FRONTLINE

*E*ach year in late September, The Ramp Church International dedicates a week to corporate fasting and prayer. While I maintain a personal fasting regimen, there is something profoundly transformative about a collective consecration.

It is, without question, my favorite time of the year at Ramp Church. Every consecration week is memorable, and I can trace defining moments in my life back to the spiritual preparation that took place during this sacred time.

This past consecration was nothing short of extraordinary—it truly blew my mind. The Lord spoke to me with unparalleled clarity, confirming His direction and revealing the immense increase that was about to manifest in everything I was building.

Prophetic words poured in, affirming the divine momentum fueling my assignments. I emerged from that week invigorated, charged with purpose, and ready to pursue the call of God with relentless determination.

The day after the fast, my good friend, Deacon Robert Williams, approached me with a word from God: *"There is a breach in your life, and you must address it."*

His words hit me like a ton of bricks.

In that moment, I was reminded of Moses. God had given him an assignment—to stand before Pharaoh and demand Israel's freedom. Yet immediately after Moses accepted this divine mandate, Scripture tells us that God sought to kill him.

Why? Because Moses had not circumcised his son. How could he be entrusted with God's law for an entire nation while neglecting it in his own household? Before Moses could move forward, God required him to first address the breach.

Elevation is a blessing, but it comes with its own challenges. As you rise to new levels, you will inevitably face new levels of warfare. This is why God, in His wisdom, sometimes delays certain opportunities or blessings.

It's not because He doesn't want you to have them—it's because He knows you're not ready yet.

Your walls aren't fortified, and without strong defenses, the attacks that come with elevation could crush you.

Walls symbolize protection, boundaries, and strength. In ancient times, cities were only as strong as their walls.

A breach in the wall allowed enemies to invade, plunder, and destroy.

The same is true in our lives. If there are gaps in our spiritual, emotional, or relational walls, the enemy will exploit them.

Guarding Against Breaches

The enemy often uses our weaknesses as an avenue to gain access. Whether it's an unhealed wound, weak boundaries, or unchecked emotions, those vulnerabilities can create breaches in our walls.

Leaders with a big heart for people—especially in ministry—are often targeted because of their compassion.

Many times, we see this in leadership: someone with a genuine desire to help and a nature that strives to see the best in people can become blinded to the signs of deception. The warning signs may be there, but because of our willingness to help others, we sometimes ignore what God is showing us.

The enemy knows that our emotions and good intentions can cloud our judgment, and he will exploit those areas to cause harm if our walls aren't fortified.

Anointing and Success Attract Attention

Anointing and success draw people, but not all of them have good intentions. Some will come because they are inspired by you and want to learn. Others will come because they believe in your vision and want to partner with you. But there are also those who are on assignment from the enemy, sent to distract, derail, or destroy you.

The enemy doesn't want you to be used by God. Remember, he was once God's instrument of worship. Because of his pride, he lost his position and place in God. Now, he hates that you are appointed by God to do what he was once called to do.

The funny thing is, the enemy is still being used by God—but not in the way he wants. God is sovereign and even uses the enemy's schemes to accomplish His purposes. Yet you must be vigilant because the enemy will do everything in his power to exploit your weaknesses and create breaches in your walls.

The Role of Offensive Linemen

To fortify your walls, think of the role of offensive linemen in football. Their job is to protect the quarterback, often considered the most valuable player on the field. Offensive linemen form a human wall, absorbing the opponent's attacks to protect the quarterback.

One of the most critical roles of an offensive lineman is protecting the quarterback's blind side—the area the quarterback can't see.

Without this protection, the quarterback becomes vulnerable to surprise attacks that can disrupt the game or even cause injury.

In the same way, you need "offensive linemen" in your life—people who stand in the gap to protect you, cover you, and defend your blind spots.

These individuals are not seeking recognition; their focus is on shielding you from harm. They help fortify your walls by praying for you, holding you accountable, and offering wise counsel.

Having the right people in your corner can mean the difference between victory and defeat.

My wife has been one of those people for me. She stands in the breach, shielding me from unseen threats and covering my vulnerabilities.

As leaders, especially pastors, our inherent desire to see the best in others can sometimes blind us to ulterior motives.

My wife has consistently provided invaluable cover, particularly in those blind spots I couldn't perceive myself. Her discernment is not just a gift—it's a shield.

Preparing for Elevation

Fortifying your walls requires preparation. God is not going to elevate you to a level that your character, discipline, or relationships cannot sustain. He's giving you time to build, strengthen, and fortify your walls.

1. Build Your Faith

Deepen your relationship with God. Spend time in prayer, fasting, and studying His Word. The stronger your spiritual foundation, the more resilient you'll be when attacks come.

2. Establish Healthy Boundaries

Protect your time, your energy, and your focus. Learn to say no to people and opportunities that don't align with your purpose.

3. Evaluate Your Circle: Surround yourself with people who strengthen your walls, not weaken them. Look for individuals who encourage, challenge, and push you to grow. Trust your discernment

—believe people when they show you who they are. Don't promote anyone into your circle without spiritual examination.

4. Strengthen Your Weak Areas

Be honest with yourself about your vulnerabilities. Seek mentorship, counseling, or resources to address those areas before you step into the next season.

5. Guard Your Heart

Proverbs 4:23 reminds us, *"Above all else, guard your heart, for everything you do flows from it."* Protect your emotions by seeking God's wisdom before making decisions about people or opportunities.

The Purpose of the Walls

Strong walls aren't just for keeping the enemy out—they're also for protecting the blessings within. God wants you to walk in abundance, but He also wants you to be able to sustain it.

He's preparing you not just for success, but for longevity.

Consider Nehemiah, called to rebuild the walls of Jerusalem. The process required focus, resilience, and teamwork. Nehemiah faced opposition, but he stayed committed to the work because he understood its importance.

In the same way, you must remain committed to strengthening your foundation, trusting that God is preparing you for greater things and ensuring that nothing hinders your progress.

Reflection

- What gaps or weaknesses in your life might the enemy be using to gain access?
- Who in your life serves as an "offensive lineman," protecting you from harm and covering your blind spots?

- What steps can you take to ensure your walls are fortified?

Prayer

Father,

Thank You for being my protector and fortifying my walls. I ask for discernment to identify any gaps in my defenses and for wisdom to strengthen those areas. Surround me with the right people who will protect me, guide me, and hold me accountable.

Help me to guard my heart, my mind, and my spirit so that I can walk in the purpose You have for me. Keep me humble and vigilant as I prepare for the elevation You have planned. Thank You for the anointing and favor You have placed on my life, and help me to steward it wisely.

In Jesus' name, Amen.

26

ILLUMINATE THE PATH

Have you ever walked out of a meeting feeling more confused than when you walked in because there was no clear agenda? Or found yourself on a team where everyone was moving but had no clear direction? Or maybe you've been in a situation where multiple voices gave conflicting instructions, leaving you stuck and frustrated instead of moving forward?

A lack of clarity is a silent killer. Marriages crumble when spouses aren't aligned on their vision for the future. Ministries struggle when leaders fail to communicate the mission effectively. Businesses collapse when teams are left guessing instead of executing with purpose.

An unclear or poorly communicated vision doesn't just slow progress—it breeds frustration, confusion, and even division. People can't follow what they don't understand. And without a shared vision, even the most talented teams, the strongest relationships, and the most anointed ministries will struggle to thrive.

Clarity isn't a luxury; it's a necessity. Where there is vision, there is momentum. Where there is clear direction, there is success.

One of the most powerful tools for fulfilling your purpose is the ability to illuminate the path—clearly and compellingly communicating your vision.

The Bible speaks about the importance of vision in Proverbs 29:18: *"Where there is no vision, the people perish."* Vision, in its simplest form, provides direction.

It inspires action and aligns hearts and efforts. However, communicating that vision in a way that others truly understand and buy into it is a challenge.

Communication is often seen as a simple exchange of information, but the reality is much more complex. Just because you think you've communicated your vision clearly doesn't mean it has been understood in the way you intended.

The Disconnect: Thinking You've Communicated vs. Actually Communicating

In life and in ministry, we often assume that people "get" what we're saying or what we mean. Perhaps we've spoken our thoughts aloud, shared our hopes, or even outlined our plans.

But the fact is, the perception of communication is not the same as true communication. What we say may not always be what others hear or understand.

This disconnect between what you say and what they hear can lead to frustration, misalignment, and missed opportunities.

The issue isn't that people aren't listening—it's that they may not fully understood your vision or its heart. This gap can be costly in relationships, work, ministry, and in fulfilling your calling.

Consider the frustration of a leader who has cast a compelling vision for a project, only to find that those under their leadership have misunderstood key aspects.

People may be moving in different directions or making decisions that don't align with the intended goals.

In the leader's mind, the vision was clear; but in reality, the communication of that vision was not effective.

. . .

The Impact of Unclear Communication

The consequences of unclear communication can be significant. Not only does it lead to confusion and disarray, but it also causes discouragement among those involved. Imagine a ministry leader sharing a vision for outreach, but not fully articulating the how and the why.

Volunteers may be eager, but they lack direction. Without understanding the bigger picture, they might lack motivation—or worse, they may start working at cross purposes.

Similarly, in the workplace or in any collaborative environment, when the vision is not communicated clearly, efforts can become fragmented. People may misunderstand the priorities, leading to wasted time, resources, and energy. Worse, relationships can suffer as frustration builds.

The Apostle Paul, in his letters, often emphasized the importance of clear communication, especially when it came to vision and purpose. He wrote in 1 Corinthians 14:8, *"For if the trumpet makes an uncertain sound, who will prepare for battle?"*

A call to action that is unclear or uncertain does not inspire a unified response. In essence, when your vision is not communicated clearly, it can create a "trumpet sound" that leads to confusion, disarray, and missed opportunities.

The Elements of Effective Communication

Effective communication is not just about talking; it's about making sure the message is received and understood as you intend. Here are some principles that will help you bridge the gap between your vision and others' understanding:

1. Clarity of Purpose

Before you can communicate your vision clearly to others, you need to be clear on what the vision is. Take time to define your purpose, refine your message, and ensure that it is simple and focused.

2. Consistent Messaging

Communicating your vision once is rarely enough. Consistency is key. People need to hear your vision repeatedly, from different angles and in various formats. Repetition helps people internalize the message, and it strengthens their commitment.

3. Active Listening

Effective communication is a two-way street. Clearly share your vision, but also listen to feedback. Open dialogue builds trust, clarifies your message, and ensures understanding. Actively listening allows you to refine and align your vision more effectively.

4. Call to Action

A vision should never be communicated without a clear call to action. People need to know what they're supposed to do with the vision. Simply hearing about your hopes and dreams is inspiring, but it's not enough. Provide clear steps, responsibilities, and expectations so that everyone knows how they can contribute.

Vision without Communication Leads to Division

Your vision is powerful—but only when communicated effectively. The problem isn't that you have a vision; the problem often lies in assuming you've communicated it clearly when, in fact, you haven't. Clear, intentional communication is vital to ensure that everyone involved understands the purpose, the path forward, and their role in it.

Remember, you are not just sharing a dream or a goal; you are calling others to align with God's greater purpose. When you communicate that vision with clarity, consistency, and care, you invite others to be part of the story God is writing through your life. Most importantly, communicate with the intention of creating understanding, connection, and action.

Your vision has the power to change lives—but only if you communicate it in a way that others can hear, grasp, and act upon it. If you can illuminate the path, the people will follow you!

Reflection
- How clear is your vision for your life or ministry? Have you taken the time to define, refine, and effectively communicate it to those around you?
- Have you ever assumed someone understood your vision only to realize they didn't? How could you have communicated the vision effectively?
- When you share your vision, do you also give others a clear, actionable next step? How do you ensure everyone knows their role in bringing the vision to life?

Prayer
Father,

Thank You for the vision You have placed in my heart. I pray for clarity and wisdom in articulating this vision to others. Help me communicate with purpose, consistency, and love so that those around me clearly understand and align with Your calling.

I ask for Your Holy Spirit to guide my words, remove any barriers to understanding, and open hearts to receive the message You want to deliver. Lord, I also pray for active listening in my conversations, that I may hear the concerns and feedback of others with humility and openness. May my communication build connection, trust, and unity.

In Jesus' name, Amen.

27

I'M IN IT BUT IT'S NOT IN ME

As we journey through life, we inevitably encounter various cultures—whether in a new job, a different church, or a new community. Each of these environments has its unique set of values, behaviors, and expectations that can impact how we think, act, and relate to others.

While it is important to adapt and become effective within the culture we find ourselves in, there is a subtle danger: the risk of losing our personal identity in the process.

One day, during my internship at Bad Boy Entertainment, my director called me into her office. She put everything on pause, locked eyes with me, and said, *"As much as I want to keep you here, I know your heart is set on acting and filmmaking. You need to move to L.A., but just know—most people sell their souls to make it out there."*

At the time, I didn't fully grasp the weight of her words—but years later, I would.

Fueled by ambition and armed with big dreams, I took her advice and made the move. But I wasn't prepared for the lifestyle, the allure, or the temptations that awaited me.

Little by little, I lost sight of who I was. The lines I swore I'd never cross became blurred. The industry didn't just surround me—it consumed me. I became someone I no longer recognized.

The statement, *"Maintain individualism as you acclimate to a culture,"* challenges us to find a balance between fitting into a new environment and staying true to who God created us to be.

The Apostle Paul, in his letter to the Romans, encourages believers not to conform to the ways of this world, but to allow their minds to be transformed by the renewing power of Christ. This transformation allows us to understand God's will and live in a way that aligns with His purpose for us.

Recognize Your Unique Calling

The first step in maintaining individualism in the face of new cultural influences is recognizing that you are uniquely created by God with a purpose. Your personality, passions, and experiences reflect God's design for you. While cultures may have collective values and expectations, God calls each person individually to serve His Kingdom in a unique way.

When you know who you are in Christ, you can confidently engage with the culture around you without losing sight of your identity. Just as Jesus walked through different cities, meeting people from all walks of life, He never compromised His values. He maintained His mission and His message while engaging with various cultural contexts.

Transform, Not Conform

It's easy to fall into the trap of conforming to the patterns of a new environment, particularly when you desire to fit in or be accepted. Conformity, however, can lead to the erosion of our uniqueness.

Instead, Paul urges us to be transformed through the renewal of our minds. This renewal happens when we allow the Holy Spirit to reshape our thinking and actions, aligning them with God's will rather than the world's.

Being transformed is not about resisting change; it's about being influenced by God's Word and His Spirit rather than by the pressures of external culture.

As you adjust to new surroundings, ask yourself: *"Is this cultural practice or behavior in alignment with God's truth?"* By allowing your mind to be renewed, you can hold on to your individual identity while navigating new spaces.

Stand Firm in Your Convictions

In any culture, you will encounter challenges that test your values and convictions. Whether in the workplace or a new community, it's essential to stand firm in the truth of God's Word. You can respect cultural differences without compromising your beliefs.

Just as Daniel in the Old Testament maintained his commitment to God while living in Babylon, you too can thrive in new environments by holding on to your identity in Christ. Daniel 1:8 says, *"But Daniel purposed in his heart that he would not defile himself."*

Daniel could have been killed. Sanctification doesn't mean you won't face tests; rather, it was his sanctification that led to his promotion.

Your sanctification may attract opposition, but it will also lead to success.

Standing firm doesn't mean being combative—it means prioritizing God's truth above all else.

When you stay true to your convictions, others may see your authenticity and be drawn to the light of Christ within you.

Engage with Wisdom and Grace

As you acclimate to a new culture, it is vital to engage with others in a way that reflects both your individuality and the grace of God.

The Bible teaches us to be *"wise as serpents and harmless as doves"* (Matthew 10:16).

This means exercising discernment when interacting with the

world. We don't compromise our beliefs, but we demonstrate kindness and understanding.

Cultural differences can sometimes lead to misunderstanding or tension. In those moments, choose grace.

Instead of conforming to the patterns of frustration or conflict, seek peaceful resolutions that reflect God's love and wisdom.

You can maintain your individuality while showing the love of Christ in a world that desperately needs it.

Grow in Your Purpose

Ultimately, the goal of maintaining individualism as you acclimate to a culture is to grow in your God-given purpose. Cultures may influence your environment, but they should not define your calling.

In every situation, God is working to refine you and shape you into the person He has called you to be. By staying rooted in Him, you can thrive wherever He places you.

Remember that your purpose isn't limited to a single cultural context. You are called to be salt and light in every culture you enter. Your individuality, shaped by God's image, will shine brightest when you walk with purpose and integrity, embracing the beauty of diversity while remaining steadfast in Christ.

God placed Joseph in Egypt, Esther in Persia, and Daniel in Babylon. They learned the world's systems but never compromised their identity.

About nine years ago, Apostle Travis Jennings prophesied to me—though we had never met before. He walked over, leaned in, and whispered in my ear:

"The Lord is sending you back to Hollywood, but this time, He will keep you holy. You'll be in it, but it won't be in you."

Those words have stayed with me ever since. Now, the first script is almost ready. Stay tuned—God's plan is unfolding. I won't lose myself this time!

. . .

Reflection
- How have you struggled to maintain your identity in a new cultural environment?
- Are there areas in which you've compromised your beliefs to fit in? How can you re-establish your convictions in a godly way?
- How can you show grace and wisdom in a culture that differs from your own while staying true to your calling?

Prayer

Father,

Thank You for creating me uniquely and giving me purpose. Help me to maintain my individual identity as I engage with the cultures. Transform my mind and my heart through Your Word, that I may live in a way that honors You. Give me the strength to stand firm in my convictions while engaging with others in love and grace. May I shine Your light in every culture I encounter, growing in the purpose You have set before me.

In Jesus' name, Amen.

28

REPRESENTATION MATTERS

In 2018, H&M—a globally recognized clothing brand—found itself embroiled in a public relations crisis after releasing an advertisement featuring a black child wearing a sweatshirt with the words *"coolest monkey in the jungle"* emblazoned across the front.

The fallout was swift and intense. It wasn't just the offensive nature of the ad; it also highlighted a deeper issue: a lack of diversity in the decision-making process.

At the time, H&M's creative team was predominantly white—four white men and six white women. The failure to include diverse perspectives in the room led to a deeply problematic misstep.

While H&M has taken steps to address the issue, it serves as a glaring reminder of why diversity matters—not just in representation, but in decision-making, creativity, and building something that truly reflects the world we live in.

This incident underscores the importance of diversity, particularly in our lives, our purpose, and the teams we build. Whether it's in ministry, business, or community, we are called to embrace diversity in all its forms.

The value of having diverse voices, backgrounds, and perspectives on the table cannot be overstated—it is essential in pursuing our God-given purpose and fulfilling His mission.

The Power of Diversity in Fulfilling God's Purpose

At the heart of God's plan for humanity is diversity. We are made in God's image, and His image is not homogenous. It's a rich tapestry of diversity that reflects His creativity and glory.

The problem we often face is that we are naturally inclined to surround ourselves with people who look like us, think like us, and share similar experiences.

This can create a false sense of comfort, but it also limits our growth.

When we only engage with people who mirror our worldview, we miss out on the opportunity for growth, innovation, and deeper understanding.

God created us to live in community and to work alongside people who bring different strengths, gifts, and insights to the table.

God's Kingdom thrives on diversity. When we embrace perspectives different from our own, we gain a fuller understanding of His plan and experience growth beyond what we could have imagined.

The Importance of Gender, Ethnic, and Generational Diversity

To fulfill your purpose, it is essential to embrace not only diverse perspectives but also diversity in gender, ethnicity, and generations. For your company, church, or team to reflect the world and attract those God is calling you to serve, it must intentionally cultivate diversity.

1. Gender Diversity

Women and men bring unique perspectives and strengths to the table. From leadership to service, we see in Scripture that God has called both men and women to be active participants in His Kingdom.

Jesus treated women with the same dignity, respect, and calling to mission as He did men. Whether it's a woman like Mary Magdalene who was entrusted with the news of His resurrection, or the women who played pivotal roles in the early Church, gender diversity matters in fulfilling God's mission.

2. Ethnic Diversity

We must recognize that God's plan is for every tribe, tongue, and nation to come together in worship. We cannot fulfill the Great Commission by isolating ourselves in homogenous groups.

Ethnicities provide richness, perspective, and insight into God's diverse creation. Embracing ethnic diversity in our churches, businesses, and ministries broadens our vision and helps us more fully understand and reflect the beauty of God's creation.

3. Generational Diversity

Older generations possess wisdom and experience that can guide and mentor younger generations. Conversely, younger generations bring innovation, creativity, and fresh perspectives.

Building a team that spans multiple generations fosters both wisdom and growth, creating a space where knowledge is passed down, but new ideas are also embraced.

Your company, church, or community should reflect the diversity of the people you seek to serve. To impact a diverse world, you need a team that authentically represents it.

The Example of Jesus and His Diverse Call

When we look to the life of Jesus, we see a radical approach to diversity. Jesus didn't limit His message or His circle to a particular group of people. He sought out individuals from all walks of life to be part of His ministry. His disciples came from diverse backgrounds—

fishermen, tax collectors, zealots, and women all played integral roles in His mission.

After His resurrection, Jesus chose women—not men—as the first witnesses to His victory over death. Jesus shattered societal barriers, proving that the gospel was never meant to be confined to one group. His disciples came from different backgrounds, occupations, and perspectives, and through these differences, they were able to form a powerful, unified force that transformed the world.

When we embrace diversity, we reflect the image of God. But we must understand that embracing diversity comes with its challenges. It's not always easy.

Differences in perspective and culture can lead to tension, discomfort, and conflict. But this discomfort is where the real growth happens. When we are willing to listen to others and learn from them, we grow in our understanding, compassion, and unity.

Diversity Takes Intentionality

Building a diverse team, ministry, or community requires intentional effort. It's not enough to simply say we value diversity; we must take active steps to engage with people who are different from us. This means stepping out of our comfort zones, challenging our assumptions, and acknowledging that we don't have all the answers.

Embracing diversity requires humility—it means recognizing that we can learn something from others who bring different perspectives.

It's easy to surround ourselves with people who agree with us and look like us. But God calls us to collaborate, not compete. We are designed to complement each other. The more we work with those who are different from us, the more we grow—individually, as a team, and as a community.

God stretches us through diversity, preparing us for greater things. In our differences, we see His work unfold in powerful and unexpected ways.

. . .

Reflection:
- Does your company, church, or team reflect the diversity you seek to attract?
- What changes can you make to include more gender, ethnic, and generational diversity?
- Are there biases or comfort zones keeping you from fully embracing diversity?

Prayer

Father,

Thank You for the beautiful diversity You've created in this world. You have made us all unique, yet we are all created in Your image. Help me to see the value in every person, regardless of their gender, ethnicity, or generation. May I reflect Your love and inclusivity in the way I build relationships and pursue my purpose. Lord, give me the courage to step out of my comfort zone and embrace the diversity You have placed before me. May my company, church, or ministry reflect the richness of Your Kingdom, welcoming all people to join in Your mission.

In Jesus' name, Amen.

29

CALCULATED FAITH

In Matthew 14:22-33, the disciples found themselves in a tight situation on the Sea of Galilee. The wind was against them, and they struggled to control their boat. In the midst of the storm, they saw something unimaginable—Jesus, walking on the water toward them. At first, they were terrified, unsure of what they were seeing. But Jesus reassured them, saying, *"Take courage! It is I. Don't be afraid."*

Then Peter, ever impulsive and eager to demonstrate his faith, boldly declared, *"Lord, if it's You, command me to come to You on the water."* Jesus simply said, *"Come."*

Peter stepped out of the boat and began to walk on the water toward Jesus. But when he saw the wind and the waves, fear took over, and he began to sink. Immediately, Jesus reached out His hand and saved him, saying, *"You of little faith, why did you doubt?"*

This powerful story teaches us not just about faith, but about the necessity of calculated faith. It teaches us about a faith that is not reckless or impulsive, but is rooted in a deep understanding of God's will and direction.

Peter's step out of the boat wasn't just boldness—it was obedience. Calculated faith means stepping out only when Jesus invites you.

Faith isn't about testing God or acting on impulse; it's about aligning with His will and stepping forward in obedience.

Peter didn't just decide one day to walk on water because it sounded like a good idea. He asked Jesus, *"If it's You, tell me to come to You on the water."* Peter understood that he couldn't do it on his own; it was only by Jesus' command that the impossible became possible. When Jesus told him to come, Peter's faith was calculated and based on the Word of God. It wasn't a leap of foolishness; it was a step of obedience, based on Jesus' invitation.

Calculated Faith: Trusting God's Timing and Direction

Calculated faith requires more than just believing that God can do the impossible—it involves waiting for His direction and trusting in His timing. When we step out in faith, we must ensure that it is God who is leading us, rather than our own desires or assumptions. There are many things in life that can look like opportunities, but not all of them are God-ordained. Just because something seems possible doesn't mean it's God's plan for you.

For instance, some people quit their jobs or move to a new city, claiming "faith," yet they lack a clear word from God. They say, *"I'm trusting God will provide,"* but in reality, God never told them to make that leap. This kind of reckless faith can lead to frustration and hardship when it is based on our own impulses rather than a clear direction from God. True faith doesn't involve moving ahead without God's invitation—it involves moving with God, at His pace and according to His plans.

The Danger of Walking Without God's Invitation

Peter began to sink the moment he shifted his focus from Jesus to the storm. As long as his eyes were on Jesus, he was able to defy natural laws. But when his focus shifted, doubt crept in, and he began to sink. Calculated faith means keeping your focus on Jesus, even when the waves of life seem overwhelming.

Stepping out without God's invitation can lead to unnecessary danger, confusion, and frustration. Faith is not about making decisions on your own and hoping that God will bless them. It's about moving in sync with His voice and obeying His Word, even when your circumstances seem uncertain.

Reckless faith can sometimes be mistaken for boldness, but true boldness in Christ comes with a Holy Ghost unction.

Faith in Action: Moving with Jesus, Not Without Him

Faith without action leads to passive waiting, but action without faith is reckless. When God calls you to step out, it's not just about boldness—it's about ensuring your actions align with His will. God desires to see calculated faith in action, faith that is strategic, intentional, and anchored in His truth.

Walking in obedience means relying not on our strength or wisdom, but on Jesus—the only One who sustains us.

The Power of Obedient Faith

When we look at Peter's story, we see that even though he faltered momentarily, Jesus reached out and saved him. Calculated faith is not about never making mistakes or feeling fear—it's about trusting in Jesus' ability to save and sustain us, even when we fall.

When God calls you, perfection is not required—obedience is. What matters is your willingness to keep your eyes on Him, trust in His plan, and get back up when you stumble.

Jesus didn't condemn Peter for his fear; He addressed the lack of faith in that moment, but He still reached out and lifted Peter. Even when we step out in faith and falter, He will be there to catch us.

Living with Calculated Faith

Calculated faith means knowing that you can't walk on water unless Jesus tells you to come. It's about moving when He says move, standing still when He says wait, and trusting that His timing, direction, and provision will be there for you every step of the way.

Calculated faith rests in the assurance that God's voice is our ultimate authority. When we follow Him, we move in confidence, knowing He sustains us every step of the way.

As you step out in faith, ask yourself: Is this what God is calling me to? Don't walk on water unless Jesus bids you to come. When He calls, nothing is impossible. But remember, the power to walk on water comes not from your ability, but from His Word, His calling, and your obedience.

Step out in faith—but let it be calculated faith, rooted in obedience, trust, and the unshakable confidence that Jesus is with you.

Reflections

- Have you ever stepped out in faith without hearing from God first? What were the results?
- How does "calculated faith" apply to your life right now? Are you waiting on God's direction or trying to make things happen on your own?
- What steps of obedience can you take today to align with God's calling and purpose?

Prayer

Father,

Thank You for Peter's example, showing us that faith rooted in Your voice leads to victory. Help me trust Your timing and direction, not moving ahead in my own strength or impulsive desires. I surrender my plans and seek Your clarity and wisdom in every decision. When fear creeps in or storms overwhelm me, remind me to keep my eyes on You. May my faith be anchored in obedience and trust, knowing You are with me every step of the way.

In Jesus' name, Amen.

30

THE PARADOX OF PERFECTION: TRUSTING GOD THROUGH IMPERFECTION

If you look at the list of timeless classics on IMDb (International Movie Database), you'll see that many of the movies we consider legendary are far from perfect. *The Godfather*, often hailed as one of the greatest films of all time, includes a fight scene in which a punch is clearly missed.

The Color Purple, another beloved classic, features a clip-on tie in a scene set in 1916, despite clip-on ties not being invented until 1928. And in *Casablanca*, a scene shows Rick and Sam boarding a train after standing in the rain, but their coats are mysteriously dry.

It's fascinating, isn't it? These films, though filled with moments of brilliance, carry their imperfections—and yet, they still endure, still hold a place of honor in the cinematic world. Why?

Because the message, the artistry, and the heart behind them transcended those minor mistakes. Even masterpieces aren't flawless—and that's okay.

We, too, are often in the process of creating something great—whether it's a book, a song, a business, a ministry, or a life. But so many times, we hold back from releasing what we've been working on because we want it to be perfect. We wait for the right moment, the right amount of preparation, the right conditions, believing that the key to success is flawless execution.

But in reality, perfection is often an illusion. In striving for flawlessness, we risk missing the opportunity to share what God has placed within us.

The Paradox of Perfection

Perfectionism is a trap. While we strive for excellence, we can become so consumed by the idea of achieving a perfect result that we fail to act at all. We might convince ourselves that we aren't ready, that our work isn't good enough, or that we need to make just one more tweak. But the truth is, God doesn't expect perfection from us.

He expects obedience. He wants us to release what He has put inside us, flaws and all, because there is purpose in our imperfections.

The beauty of creation—whether a movie, a song, a business, or even our lives—lies not in perfection but in the willingness to move forward despite imperfections. When we release what God has given us, even if it's not perfect, we trust Him to work through our imperfections. His strength is perfected in our weakness. When we surrender our flaws to Him, they become part of the masterpiece He is crafting.

Trusting God to Work Through Imperfection

There comes a point in every project, every dream, every endeavor, when you have to take a step of faith and let go. Even though it may not be perfect, even though it may not be exactly as you envisioned, there is a release that must happen. Trust God to take what you've done, imperfections and all, and use it for His glory.

When you think about it, God Himself didn't create us to be flawless. He made us in His image, but He also gave us free will, which means we are capable of making mistakes. Yet, despite our flaws, He still calls us His masterpiece. So why should we hold back the gifts He's placed in us just because we're worried about getting it "right"?

If God required perfection before using us, nothing would ever be accomplished. Just like a classic movie, your work, your dream, your purpose will have imperfections—but those imperfections don't disqualify you. They don't make your offering any less valuable. In fact, they may be exactly what makes it relatable and impactful to others.

Release What God Has Put in You

At some point, we must accept that perfection will never be fully realized on this side of eternity. But that doesn't mean we shouldn't strive for excellence and give our best. It simply means that we must release what we have, trust God to do the rest, and be okay with the fact that it might not be perfect.

We often fear what people will think—will they see our mistakes? Will they notice the flaws we wish we had corrected? But the reality is, most people aren't looking for perfection. They're looking for authenticity. They're looking for something real, something they can connect with. Your imperfections don't weaken your message—they often strengthen it.

So, what has God placed in you that you've been hesitant to release?

- A book you've been writing but are afraid isn't quite good enough?
- A business idea that you've been overanalyzing instead of launching?
- A ministry you feel called to start but are waiting for the "perfect" time?
- A song, a sermon, a project, a dream you've kept hidden because you fear it won't measure up?

Don't be imprisoned by perfectionism. It is a heavy burden that can hold you back from fully stepping into what God has called you to do. Perfectionism whispers lies that say you are not ready, that your work is not good enough, that you must fix every flaw before you can move forward. But God never asked for perfection—He asked for surrender. He asked for a willing heart that trusts Him more than the fear of imperfection.

When you release the need to have everything just right, you make room for God to move. You allow Him to shape and refine not just your work, but also your heart. The masterpiece He is creating is not just about what you produce; it's about who you are becoming in the process.

Every mistake, every lesson learned, every imperfection is woven into the greater story He is telling through your life. Your perceived flaws and missteps do not diminish the beauty of what He is creating; they enhance it.

Let go of the pressure to be perfect. Step forward with confidence, trusting that God will take what you offer—unfinished as it may be—and transform it into something extraordinary. Trust that God will weave your imperfections into the greater masterpiece He is painting in your life.

May you receive the Master's peace, knowing that even with your imperfections, He is still at work, crafting something beautiful.

Reflection
- Is there something that God has placed in your heart that you've hesitated to release because it's not "perfect"? How can you take a step of faith and release it anyway?
- How can you view imperfection as part of God's plan for your life and your work?
- What does it mean to trust God to use your flaws for His glory?

Prayer
Father,
Thank You for giving me purpose and vision. I know You don't

require perfection—only a willing heart. Help me trust You in the process, release the need for perfection, and step forward in faith. Use my imperfections for Your glory, and remind me that You are always at work in and through me.

In Jesus' name, Amen.

UNPACK HERE

We often hear sermons about enduring the process and weathering the storm. But God doesn't leave us in the middle forever—there is always a day of breakthrough. One day, you will marry the person God has ordained for you. One day, your church or business will thrive. One day, your book, film, or music will be released and impact the world. One day, it will happen!

After years of survival mode and constant transition, we may feel unsettled even when we finally reach the place we've fought so hard for. It's like someone returning home after years in prison—unsure how to embrace freedom, still looking over their shoulder, uncertain how to live in their new reality. But the truth is, you are in a new place now. God has brought you here to rest, to flourish, and to enjoy the blessings He's prepared for you.

It's the moment you realize your past battles no longer define you, and you're standing at the threshold of a new season—one of promise, victory, and fulfillment.

In this new season, remember this: you made it. You've crossed over from the struggle into the promise. God is calling you to unpack your life, to plant roots, and to fully embrace the place He has prepared for you. Yes, challenges will come, but they will be new challenges, met with new strength. This is a season of peace, purpose, and provision like you've never experienced before. Don't just survive—live.

The Day the Manna Stopped: A New Day Is Coming

Joshua 5:12 tells us that *"the manna stopped the day after the Israelites ate food from the land."* For 40 years, God had provided for His people with manna in the wilderness. Every morning, they gathered the miraculous bread from heaven, but once they entered the Promised Land and ate the produce of the land, the manna ceased.

This marked a shift—a clear sign that they had arrived in the land of promise.

Similarly, for you, there will be a day when your spiritual manna stops. The days of wilderness provision are over. A new season of abundance has arrived. Your appetite should change because you are no longer living on yesterday's miracle.

God is preparing you to feast on the fruits of your labor, the fruits of His promises.

Just as the Israelites transitioned from manna to harvest, you must shift from surviving to thriving. The fight is ending.

You Are in Your Promised Land: Rest and Unpack

When you reach this new place—this season of promise—it's not just about surviving. It's about resting.

It's time to unpack.

You're not meant to just pass through this season; you're meant to settle in and enjoy the fulfillment of what God has promised. This is the land flowing with milk and honey, the land where your soul can finally rest, knowing that God is faithful to His Word.

You've endured the battles, the waiting, and the longing. Now, it's time to step fully into your breakthrough.

The key here is to understand that you can rest in this place and unpack your life.

The Israelites' Turning Point: "You Shall See Them No More Forever"

In Exodus 14:13-14, Moses spoke these words to the Israelites:

"Do not be afraid. Stand firm and you will see the deliverance the Lord will bring you today. The Egyptians you see today, you will never see again."

These words were not only for the Israelites standing at the Red Sea, but also for you. The struggles, the enemies, and challenges of your past will not follow you into this new season.

The bondage of Egypt—your past struggles, hurts, and regrets—has been left behind. You will not have to face that fight again. God's deliverance is final.

Whatever held you in the past, whatever caused you to live in fear, regret, or anxiety, will no longer have a claim on your future. You are free. You have crossed over.

The war is over, the battle is won, and now, victory is yours to embrace. Step boldly into your breakthrough—this is your moment to rejoice!

Unpack Your Promise: Settle into Your Blessings

When the Israelites entered the Promised Land, they didn't just camp at the border—they moved in, they unpacked, and they settled into their inheritance. The land was theirs, and it was time to enjoy it. Similarly, in this new season, it's time for you to unpack your promises.

Unpacking isn't just about settling physically—it's about anchoring your heart in the truths of God's promises. This is a season to unpack your faith, your peace, your joy, and your vision.

Unpack your confidence in God's provision and His ability to bring everything He promised to fruition.

Just like you wouldn't move into a new house without unpacking your belongings, don't move into your new season of promise without unpacking everything that God has in store for you.

Live fully in His blessings. Don't leave any area of your life untouched by His grace.

Your New Season is Not Just For You—It's Meant to Flow Through You

It's essential to remember that the promises of God are not just for you—they are also meant to flow through you to others. This new season of blessing is not just for your personal fulfillment, but for the greater purpose God has for your life. Your faith, your testimony, and your victory will inspire and bless those around you.

You have been called to be a conduit of God's goodness. As you walk into your new season, others will see God's faithfulness in your life and be drawn to the hope you have in Christ.

God is preparing you not just for personal breakthrough, but also for a kingdom purpose. He will use you in this new season to bless others, to encourage them, and to lead them into their own seasons of promise.

Move Forward in Faith

As you step fully into this new place, remember the words spoken to the Israelites: *"The Egyptians you see today, you will never see again."* The battles of your past are over, and now you are walking into a new season of purpose, promise, and fulfillment.

Embrace it. Trust God fully. Let go of the past and step forward, knowing that your future is secure in Him. Unpack your promise, because this is where you belong. This is where you are meant to stay. Here, God will continue to bless you, elevate you, and use you for His glory.

Reflection

- What parts of your past are you still holding on to? How can you release them and fully embrace the new season God has for you?

- How can you deepen your trust in God as you step walk into this new place He has prepared?
- What practical steps can you take to "unpack" your promise and fully live in the blessings of this new season?

Prayer

Father,

Thank You for bringing me into this season of promise. I release my past and embrace the future You have prepared for me. Help me to fully step into the blessings You've laid before me. May I walk in Your peace, provision, and purpose. I trust that You are using this season for Your glory, and I am ready to thrive in all that You have for me.

In Jesus' name, Amen.

ACKNOWLEDGMENTS

To God be all the glory! Every step of this journey is a testament to Your unfailing grace and divine purpose. I stand in awe of Your faithfulness—thank You, Jesus! You have been my anchor in every storm, my light in every dark place, and my strength when I had none left. Every victory belongs to You.

To my love, my heart, my joy—my wife, Ashley. You are my answered prayer and my safe place. Your patience, wisdom, and quiet strength have carried me when I could not carry myself. I am a better man because of you, and I will spend every day thanking God for the honor of loving you and being loved by you.

To my daughter—my princess, Gabrielle. You are living proof of God's goodness in my life. Watching you grow and witnessing the fire of purpose already stirring in you is one of my greatest joys. My prayer is that you will always walk boldly in the calling God has placed upon your life, knowing that you are fearfully and wonderfully made.

Mom, your unwavering faith, unshakable strength, and boundless love have molded me into the person I am today. Your prayers, sacrifices, and belief in me have been my foundation. I will always strive to honor the legacy of faith and resilience you have instilled in me. Dad, I love you, and I thank God for you.

To my sisters—my rock-solid crew and my fiercest protectors. Your love, support, and loyalty mean everything to me. No matter where life takes us, our bond is unshakable. I treasure you more than words can express.

Bishop S.Y. Younger, words will never be enough to express my gratitude for your covering, leadership, and example. You have not only shaped my ministry but have transformed my understanding of servanthood, excellence, and integrity. Generations will walk in the paths you are blazing.

Pastor William Westgate and Lady Westgate, the dynamic duo. Pastor Westgate, it is an honor to serve alongside you. I deeply appreciate your friendship, humor, and encouragement. Lady Westgate, your guidance, insight, and tireless support have been instrumental in bringing this book to life. Your patience and wisdom have made all the difference.

To my Ramp Church International family—you are not just a congregation; you are my home, my tribe, my lifeline. Your passion for God, relentless pursuit of purpose, and dedication to excellence inspire me every single day. I am beyond blessed to serve alongside you, to worship with you, and to do life with you.

To Bad Boy Entertainment and Naa'ila Entertainment—you were more than an experience; you were a proving ground and a launchpad. You took a young boy from Jamaica, Queens, and expanded his vision beyond what he ever thought possible. You showed me that the world was bigger than I imagined and that greatness required sacrifice. For that, I am forever grateful.

To every person I have the privilege of calling family and friend—there are too many to name, but each of you holds a special place in my heart. I celebrate you, I honor you, and I thank God for you. I am blessed to be around extraordinary people. Your resilience, passion, and purpose remind me daily that we are all called to something far greater than ourselves. I am deeply grateful to walk this journey with you, and I pray that as we continue forward, we uplift and encourage one another to reach even greater heights.

With a heart overflowing with gratitude,
Marvin St. Macary

ABOUT THE AUTHOR

Marvin St. Macary's life is a masterful tapestry of transformation, woven with creativity, resilience, and an unwavering sense of purpose. From the heart of the entertainment industry to the pulpit, his journey stands as a testament to the power of divine calling and the relentless pursuit of excellence in every endeavor.

A graduate of Fordham University at Lincoln Center, Marvin earned a Bachelor's degree in Theater Arts and African American Studies. As a sophomore, Marvin secured a coveted internship at Bad Boy Entertainment and Arista Records, working in the executive offices of Sean "P. Diddy" Combs. This rare opportunity immersed him in the fast-paced world of music, fashion, and event production, granting him invaluable insights into high-level business operations.

His trajectory continued its rise when he joined Naa'ila Entertainment, serving as Executive Assistant to the legendary director Hype Williams. Quickly ascending to Assistant Producer, Marvin played a key role in the production of groundbreaking music videos for global superstars such as Jay-Z, Kanye West, and Beyoncé.

Yet, in 2006, amid the flashing lights, Marvin experienced a profound spiritual awakening—a divine call that led him to exchange the entertainment industry for full-time ministry. Relocating to Lynchburg, Virginia, he became part of Ramp Church International, where his dedication to faith, leadership, and community impact flourished.

By 2012, Marvin was ordained as a Deacon under One Way Churches International, and by 2014, he was elevated to the office of

Elder. That same year, under the leadership of Bishop S.Y. Younger, he was installed as the Executive Pastor of Ramp Church International—a role in which he has faithfully served for over a decade.

Renowned for his ability to cultivate leaders and impart profound biblical insights, Marvin bridges deep theological truths with practical application, empowering individuals to grow spiritually, personally, and professionally.

Yet, he never abandoned his artistic roots. As Executive Pastor, Marvin seamlessly integrated the arts with ministry, writing, directing, and starring in *The Witness*—a theatrical production inspired by William Seymour and the Azusa Street Revival

Never one to remain stagnant, Marvin expanded his leadership into entrepreneurial and real estate ventures. Recently earning an MBA in Marketing from Liberty University, he now oversees Ramp Church's daily ministries and business operations, playing a pivotal role in advancing its vision.

Beyond ministry and business, Marvin is a creative force in his own right. He is the founder of M. Saint Photography and co-owner of The Saint Collection, a streetwear brand built alongside his wife, Ashley, and their daughter, Gabrielle. More than just fashion, The Saint Collection is a movement—blending faith, culture, and creative expression.

Marvin is also a highly sought-after life skills speaker, equipping thousands of high school students with the tools they need to navigate the transition into successful adulthood. With a dynamic and relatable approach, he empowers young minds with practical wisdom, real-world strategies, and invaluable life lessons, helping them step confidently into their futures.

In April 2024, Marvin added the title of author to his impressive résumé with the release of *Face to Face: Conversations with My Younger Self*. Co-written with four friends, this deeply personal and thought-provoking book explores faith, destiny, and self-discovery, offering readers a reflective journey through life's defining moments.

Marvin St. Macary is more than a pastor, entrepreneur, and

creative—he is a visionary, a bridge between worlds, and a living testament to the transformative power of faith and purpose.

For more books and updates:
   www.stmacaryig.com

ALSO BY MARVIN ST. MACARY

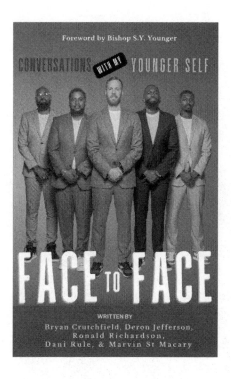

Face to Face Conversations With My Younger Self

Made in the USA
Columbia, SC
13 March 2025